FIELDWORK
WITH
CHILDREN

D0931763

For Richard, my husband and very best friend

FIELDWORK
WITH
CHILDREN

Robyn M. Holmes

SAGE Publications
International Educational and Professional Publisher
Thousand Oaks   London   New Delhi

For information:

SAGE Publications, Inc.
2455 Teller Road
Thousand Oaks, California 91320
E-mail: order@sagepub.com

SAGE Publications Ltd.
6 Bonhill Street
London EC2A 4PU
United Kingdom

SAGE Publications India Pvt. Ltd.
M-32 Market
Greater Kailash I
New Delhi 110 048 India

Printed in the United States of America
Library of Congress Cataloging-in-Publication Data

Holmes, Robyn M.
    Fieldwork with children / by Robyn M. Holmes.
        p.   cm.
    Includes bibliographical references (p.   ) and index.
    ISBN 0-7619-0754-8 (cloth: acid-free paper). —
    ISBN 0-7619-0755-6 (pbk.: acid-free paper)
        1. Children—Cross-cultural studies. 2. Children—Research—
    Methodology. 3. Ethnology—Field work. I. Title.
    GN482.H65 1998
    305.23'07'23—dc21

This book is printed on acid-free paper.

98 99 00 01 02 03 10 9 8 7 6 5 4 3 2 1

Acquiring Editor:	Peter Labella
Editorial Assistant:	Corinne Pierce
Production Editor:	Sherrise M. Purdum
Production Assistant:	Lynn Miyata
Typesetter/Designer:	Christina M. Hill
Cover Designer:	Candice Harman
Print Buyer:	Anna Chin

Contents

Preface

The position of qualitative research in the scholarly community has changed over the years. Historically, qualitative methods were associated exclusively with anthropologists and sociologists. By contrast, experimentation and scientific rigor were linked to psychologists, based in part on the discipline's historical alignment with the physical sciences.

In the past, the two methods were viewed as antithetical. The quantitative approach included an element of control over the environment and the ability to make causal statements about the relationships between variables. Issues of reliability and validity became the hallmark of this method. Qualitative methods were viewed as descriptive, with their value resting in the ability to generate hypotheses. Further distinctions noted that quantitative methods regularly used artificial settings where participants were likened to objects. In comparison, qualitative methods were used in naturalistic settings, and participants were viewed as individuals.

Current views of qualitative and quantitative methods acknowledge that these methods are alternative ways of knowing about groups or individuals. Neither method is superior—rather, each has an important contribution to make to our understanding of human behavior and cognition. Some researchers prefer to use one method exclusively, whereas others find power in using them in combination.

Researchers from diverse disciplines now use qualitative methods. Most studies are undertaken with adult individuals and groups. As Goodwin (1997) and other researchers note, field studies with child participants are relatively uncommon, however. This is attributable in part to the western notion that children are not active creators of culture. Rather, one can draw parallels to Tylor's (1871/1958) notion of cultural evolution insofar as children and childhood socialization are viewed as a stepping-stone or transitional state to adulthood, with little or no extrinsic or intrinsic value of its own.

Such asymmetry is evident in the methods literature. There are numerous works on research and qualitative methods, but only several address methodological issues with child participants. These include excellent resources by Fine and Sandstrom (1988), Pellegrini (1996), and Graue and Walsh (in press). These works emphasize the mechanics and more traditional concerns of how to conduct fieldwork with children, however. Few if any works have explored how factors such as a fieldworker's personal attributes (e.g., gender and ethnicity) affect the process with children. Although these issues have been brought to light in fieldwork with adult participants, such reflexive concerns remain relatively unexplored in fieldwork with child participants.

This work stems from this need to address gender and ethnicity issues in fieldwork with children. When I originally began my fieldwork with children, I took a gender-neutral position and presumed that male and female fieldworkers went about their business in a similar manner. I never considered the effect that these personal attributes might have on the process. After numerous conversations with colleagues about my field experiences and reading the ethnographic literature, I realized that these factors had in some way guided my fieldwork with children. In some cases, these factors were influential in a minute way; in other instances, their influence was more profound. This book is a beginning—a reconnaissance into the fieldwork process with children, which is underexplored. My hope is that it stimulates discussion and dialogue between all individuals who engage in qualitative methods, in particular in fieldwork with children.

The book should be easily digested by undergraduate and graduate students in qualitative research and methods courses. It could also be used as a supplemental text in courses on cross-cultural studies, early childhood education, and gender studies. May those who conduct fieldwork with child participants continue to improve on this process to benefit the children who graciously allow us to enter their social and cognitive realms.

Acknowledgments

Although fieldwork is a solitary endeavor, one rarely writes alone. Various people greatly influenced the final draft of this work. They include many individuals through their writings; colleagues, primary school administrators, and teachers through conversations; reviewers through their comments and suggestions; and my students through dialogues. I thank them all, for each has uniquely contributed to the final content of this book.

Monmouth University has graciously supported me in this and all my endeavors. I thank everyone at our institution who has encouraged me to improve my teaching and engage in constructive scholarship. There are two individuals to whom I owe the greatest debt. Dr. Kenneth Stunkel, dean of the School of Humanities and Social Sciences, and Dr. Doris Hiatt, chair, ex-officio, have tirelessly offered their support, encouragement, and guidance. I extend to them my sincerest appreciation for this and so much more.

I also acknowledge with appreciation the contributions of certain individuals directly involved in the making of this book; my departmental colleagues Dr. Jack Demarest, Dr. Doris Hiatt, and Dr. Janice Stapley each reviewed one or more chapters. Their influence is most noted in the gender material. Dr. Bruce Cunningham, a treasured colleague and collaborator, also reviewed several chapters. His influence is most noted in the material on gender issues and early childhood education. Their valuable and insightful comments ultimately led to further revisions of the manuscript. I kindly thank them all.

I am especially grateful to Professor Jaipaul Roopnarine for providing reading materials on East Indian and Chinese culture, and our library staff, particularly the members of the interlibrary loan and reference departments.

I extend my sincere thanks to members of the Sage community, in particular Peter Labella, editor, Corinne Pierce, editorial assistant, Sherrise M. Purdum, production editor, Lynn Miyata, production assistant, Deirdre M. Greene, copyeditor, Christina M. Hill, typesetter, Candice Harman, cover designer, and Anna Chin, print buyer. Their guidance, patience, and support was and is very much appreciated.

I also want to thank my family. My parents and siblings have always given me their love and encouragement, and my niece, Melissa, and nephews, Brian, Brian Patrick, and Kevin, have a special place in my heart. And finally, I lovingly thank my husband for the life we share and so very much more. This book is dedicated to him.

CHAPTER 1

Fieldwork With Children: An Overview

Anthropology enjoys an illustrious past that has focused on producing ethnographic accounts of non-western cultures. This emphasis on conducting fieldwork continues in the discipline today. The nature and objective of anthropology have led to a wealth of field studies and written works about adult societies. Historically, anthropology has either overlooked or neglected children's cultures. The material on children that was included in ethnographies came from peripheral observations recorded when children interacted with adults (Super & Harkness, 1986).

As Goodwin (1997, p. 1) notes, the trend to marginalize children as participants and active "creators of culture" continues. Few anthropologists have examined the life worlds of children. This is due in part to the notion that children's social

1

and cultural worlds are imperfect in comparison to the adult world they will eventually enter. Children's life experiences in their social worlds and peer cultures are presumably viewed as unimportant because the goal of socialization is to produce a culturally competent adult.

Anthropological field studies that did employ children as subjects did not emerge until the latter half of this century. Although there was a sudden surge of observational studies on children in the 1930s (Renshaw, 1981), research on children and their behaviors emerged as a worthy topic of scholarly inquiry in anthropology with the interdisciplinary Six Cultures Project (Whiting & Child, 1963; see also Mead's, 1961, work with Samoan adolescents). This extensive study examined and compared child-rearing practices in Mexico, the United States, Japan, the Philippines, Kenya, and India.

In the 1970s, children's peer cultures were investigated with renewed interest (Asher & Gottman, 1981), and anthropology eventually joined sociology, ethology, and psychology and began producing ethnographic and observational studies on children. Exceptional anthropological works include Schwartzman's (1978) work on children's play, Whiting and Whiting's (1975) cross-cultural studies on children's psychocultural and social worlds, and Middleton's (1970) and Schwartz's (1976) works on children's socialization.

Although more qualitative research with children is needed, existing field studies and other qualitative works with children from various disciplines have increased our understanding of children's behaviors and experiences substantially. For example, cross-cultural studies on children's play have revealed culture-specific and cultural universal patterns in play behaviors (e.g., Roopnarine, Johnson, & Hooper, 1994; Schwartzman, 1978). Other studies on children's play have expanded our knowledge on this topic by focusing on different contexts such as the home, school, and playground (e.g., Holmes, 1991; Kelly-Byrne, 1989; Sluckin, 1981).

Several field studies with children have examined gender issues. Exemplary works include Thorne's (1993) investigation of children's play at school and Skelton's (1996) examination of how children acquire ideas about masculinity within the school context. Social scientists have also studied peer culture in nursery schools (Corsaro, 1985), Little League baseball teams (Fine, 1987), children's ethnic knowledge (Holmes, 1995), African American children's social worlds (Goodwin, 1990), and how taking one's children into the field affects anthropological research (Butler & Turner, 1987; Cassell, 1987; Huntington, 1987).

In addition, field studies that have focused on educational issues have contributed to our understanding of children's school experiences (Andereck, 1992), day care experiences (Leavitt, 1994; J. Wolf, 1995), cross-cultural preschool experiences (Tobin, Wu, & Davidson, 1989), bilingual children's experiences in special education classrooms (Ruiz, 1995), and friendships (Rizzo, 1989).

Linguists and folklorists have contributed to our knowledge about children's verbal art forms such as rhymes and folk stories (e.g., Opie & Opie, 1984; Sutton-Smith, 1981, 1995). Other qualitative studies have expanded our knowledge about children's physical and psychological well-being in areas such as nutrition (Shu-Min, 1996), peer abuse (Ambert, 1994), family research (Daly, 1992), and health care (Bernheimer, 1986; Pass, 1987), and hospitalized children's folk perceptions of pain (Woodgate, 1996). Finally, some field studies have attempted to examine the darker aspects of childhood such as the experiences of street and homeless children (e.g., Aptekar, 1988).

In comparison to the expanding literature on qualitative studies with children, there is sparse literature that examines the fieldwork process with children. For example, qualitative researchers have been silent on issues such as how a researcher's personal attributes (e.g., gender and ethnicity) affect the fieldwork process with children. The current work addresses this need.

Subjective Issues

In the social sciences, interest in the subjective aspects of fieldwork gained prominence in the 1980s (Boros, 1988; Corsino, 1987; Kulick, 1995). Up until that time, most works were (some still are) produced without much attention given to how factors such as the motives, theoretical perspectives, and personal biases of fieldworkers affect the interpretive process and written work (Agar, 1986/1995; D. Wolf, 1996a). Van Maanen (1988) suggests that the influence of the fieldworker's emotional state, theoretical perspectives, and personal characteristics (e.g., gender, ethnicity, age, and personality) be acknowledged in the written text.

Recent works have answered the call to examine the subjective aspects of the field experience. These have primarily been conducted with adult groups (e.g., Bell, Caplan, & Karim, 1993; Birth, 1990; Fiske, 1988; Gilmore, 1991; Kleinman & Copp, 1993; Kulick & Wilson, 1995; Peshkin, 1982, 1988; Shaffir & Stebbins, 1991; Whitehead & Conaway, 1986; D. Wolf, 1996a; see also Chagnon, 1977; Holmes, 1995; Kelly-Byrne, 1989; Thorne, 1993; and Turnbull, 1968, for peripheral treatment in ethnographic works), however.

As Allum (1991) suggests, decision making during the fieldwork process is affected not just by methodological considerations. Personal, social, and emotional factors affect each stage of the fieldwork process, and these should be acknowledged in ethnographic works (see also Ellis, 1995; Kleinman & Copp, 1993; and Peshkin, 1988, for discussions on the importance of a researcher's emotions in the fieldwork process).

According to Gambell (1995), theoretical complications have arisen in ethnographies that include: a) the reverence of one's informants, b) the ethnographer's position in the study (Boxwell, 1992; Schwartzman, 1995; D. Wolf, 1996a, 1996b), and c) ethnography as text (Berger, 1993). Rosaldo (1989) advances the term *positioned subjects* to refer to actors who both participate in and conduct fieldwork. She notes that as a positioned subject, the researcher adopts a certain vantage point from which to experience and observe a group's behaviors.

These established positions and field relationships contain some element of power, and may dictate which behaviors are observed and experienced and how they are interpreted (see also D. Wolf, 1996b). Such a notion seems to be particularly salient when conducting fieldwork with children. The adult-child relationship is one that inherently implies authority. Although researchers are able to adopt roles to attenuate this (e.g., the friend role), the reality is that children are cognizant of the fieldworker's permble research personas such as classmate, friend, and grown-up. Boxwell (1992) addresses concerns about the manner in which an ethnographer inscribes himself or herself into the "text" and how this affects the written ethnographic account. Schwartzman (1995) reviews several recent ethnographies on children's play to expose some of the problems in field relationships such as researcher/informant and writer/reader that have been raised by postmodern social scientists (Clifford, 1988; Van Maanen, 1988).

Schwartzman's (1995) review of Goodwin's (1990) ethnography of African American children's social worlds addresses the fieldworker's decision to exclude participation in the field from the ethnographic text. Schwartzman notes that Goodwin adopts the realist tradition and writes herself out of the work (Van Maanen, 1988). Goodwin was an actor in the children's world, however, and the reader would benefit if Goodwin's presence and influence on the children's behavior were included in the text.

All the above issues have been unexplored in fieldwork with children. Thus, it seems relevant to consider such issues to advance qualitative research with them. Since the 1970s, there has been a change in attitude over the concern with method and training in anthropology; this is reflected in the current literature on methods. There is now a growing number of works on research methods in anthropology and the social sciences in general. Publications include texts on: a) qualitative research methods (Daly, 1992; Denzin & Lincoln, 1994; Mason, 1996; Patton, 1990); b) research methods in anthropology (Alasuutari, 1995; Bernard, 1994; Denzin, 1996; Pelto & Pelto, 1978; Spindler, 1970; Werner & Schoepfle, 1987); c) conducting fieldwork in educational settings (Andereck, 1992; Davies, 1994; Delamont, 1991); and d) fieldwork, participant observation, and ethnography (e.g., Agar, 1980, 1986/1995; Bernard, 1994; Denzin, 1996; Fetterman, 1989; Johnson, 1975; Shaffir & Stebbins, 1991; Shaffir, Stebbins, & Turowetz, 1980; Spradley, 1980; Warren, 1988).

Most of these works are general texts aimed broadly at how one goes about designing and undertaking particular kinds of research, however. For example, Bernard (1994) describes in detail how to prepare, conduct, and analyze field data. In addition, Bernard does so under the premise that the researcher is working with adult societies. Other texts concentrate on the technical aspects of writing (e.g., Wolcott, 1990) or field notes (e.g., Sanjek, 1990). More important, these texts do not discuss in great detail factors that can affect the fieldwork process or how to conduct research when the participants are children.

The only works that address how to conduct fieldwork with children are Draper's (1988) *Studying Children: Observing and Participating,* Fine and Sandstrom's (1988) *Knowing Children: Participant Observation With Minors,* Pellegrini's (1996) *Observing Children in Their Natural Worlds: A Methodological Primer,* Graue and Walsh's (in press), *Children in Context: Theories, Methods, and Ethics of Studying Children,* and Sieber and Sieber's (1992) peripheral work, *Social Research on Children and Adolescents: Ethical Issues.*

In addition to the general problems associated with conducting fieldwork, an investigator must confront special concerns (e.g., ethical concerns and child interviewing) when conducting fieldwork with children. Sieber and Sieber's (1992) work is useful as a guide to the ethical concerns and dilemmas that arise with children and teens, but it does not explore other aspects of fieldwork. Draper (1988) and Pellegrini (1996) are fine resources, but they are most useful as student workbooks for teaching observational methods.

Fine and Sandstrom's (1988) volume is particularly useful in that it provides information about establishing relationships with children, obtaining access to field sites, what and how much information to reveal to the children about the nature of the project, and ethical concerns, among other topics. Graue and Walsh's work (in press) addresses the need to acknowledge contextual information in interpreting children's behavior, and includes useful information on topics such as how to write field notes and how to videotape children.

In these works, however, the main focus is on the mechanics of how to conduct fieldwork with children. The factors that can assist in and guide this process with children remain unexplored. In particular, this includes the effect of the researcher's personal attributes on the fieldwork process with children.

Current trends and methodological concerns about the fieldwork process include: a) how a researcher's personal traits (e.g., gender, ethnicity, age, and social status) affect the collection and interpretation of participants' experiences (Bell et al., 1993; D. Wolf, 1996a); b) the need to address the reflexive aspects of fieldwork (e.g., Clifford, 1988; Van Maanen, 1995, discusses representational challenges in contemporary ethnography); c) the desire to conduct culture-specific studies; and d) conducting fieldwork with children. This current work contributes to the existing literature on qualitative methods by combining a discussion of two relatively unexplored topics— fieldwork with children and factors that affect this process.

As Agar (1986/1995) notes, several instances have arisen in which fieldworkers studying the same group have produced disparate accounts (see also Heider's, 1988, work on this issue). Agar advances the term *traditions* to explain these discrepancies (p. 18). Traditions include elements that the fieldworker draws on to interpret the experiences he or she is observing. Although Agar does not provide an exhaustive list, he does provide examples of traditions, including professional training, theoretical perspectives, studying the same group in different historical contexts, and personal attributes such as cultural heritage and gender. In the current work, I plan to focus on the latter two qualities—gender and ethnicity as they relate to conducting fieldwork with children.

One common factor that influences all fieldwork to a degree is the gender of the investigator (Bell et al., 1993; Butler & Turner, 1987; Divale, 1976; Golde, 1986; Warren, 1988; Werner & Schoepfle, 1987). Although this issue has recently received attention in the literature (Bell et al., 1993; Fiske, 1988; Warren, 1988; Whitehead & Conaway, 1986; D. Wolf, 1996a), the majority of studies have focused on adult communities. Few studies have addressed the issue of a researcher's gender in conducting fieldwork with children.

Gender classification is a cross-cultural construct that most members of a group employ to organize their behavior. Thus, it seems possible to conclude that male and female researchers will be treated differentially by the group members they study, and come to know and write about different aspects of the group (Warren, 1988).

In American society, the differential treatment of individuals based on gender begins in infancy. Numerous studies have demonstrated clearly that adult interactions with infants are shaped by the baby's gender (e.g., Etaugh, 1983; Huston, 1983). Differential socialization of children continues through the formative years, and research suggests that fathers in particular are inclined to engage in differential socialization practices with their children (e.g., Block, 1983; Siegal, 1987). These early experiences shape and influence the way these children perceive the world as adults.

The differential experiences of men and women (Fischer, 1986; Murphy & Murphy, 1985), access to different phenomena in a culture during the fieldwork period (Fine, 1987), and the influence of gender on fieldwork relationships (Bell et al., 1993; Berik, 1996; Hunt, 1984; McKegancy & Bloor, 1991; Warren, 1988) should support the influence a fieldworker's gender has on this process with children. This recognition will perhaps lead to an examination of contextualized knowledge gained through one's participants' experiences (Bell, 1993).

Thus, fieldworkers of different sexes may view the same culture and describe it differently within the theoretical framework of the cultural-ecological model proposed by Bronfenbrenner (1986, 1989). In this view, an individual's development and how he or she comes to acquire meaning and knowledge of the world are influenced by a hierarchy of various interlocking environments. Life experiences are shaped in part by parental socialization and child-rearing patterns as well as those deemed acceptable by a society, namely gender roles. Thus, they are susceptible to both ecological (e.g., home, school, neighborhood) and cultural (e.g., societal values, socialization and child-rearing practices, mores) factors that shape presumably an individual's development and life experiences. These experiences help determine how a person perceives the world (see Sutton-Smith, 1994, for how these affect one's research orientation).

A researcher's gender, age, social status, and ethnic membership (e.g., Bell et al., 1993; Bernard, 1994; Berik, 1996; McKegancy & Bloor, 1991; Thorne, 1993) are potential factors that could produce different life and socialization experiences and ultimately lead to different perceptions of the world. These salient factors also operate in the field. As Williams (1996) suggests, participants use personal characteristics of the fieldworker such as gender, social class, and ethnicity to assign roles to and classify the fieldworker's behaviors depending on the context of interaction.

The second factor that affects the fieldwork process is the researcher's ethnicity. Recent works in cross-cultural research have addressed the need for researchers to be cognizant of how their ethnic or cultural identity affects the research process (Helms, 1993; Pedersen, 1993; Sue, 1993). Sandra Bem's (1993) argument that gender acts as a filter through which individuals screen their interpretations and perceptions can also be applied to ethnicity.

For example, Agar (1986/1995) proffers the example of a professional meeting where western scholars misinterpreted Indian behaviors. Western scholars saw it fit to dichotomize Indian behaviors into either the sacred or the secular. Indian audience members quickly responded by stating that religion was pervasive in Indian life, and behaviors could not be neatly categorized using this antithetical pair. Thus, differences in cultural backgrounds were responsible for differing interpretations of the same group. A similar argument can be made for the influence of a fieldworker's cultural background on interpreting children's groups and behaviors.

This work discusses fieldwork with children and explores how the fieldworker's personal attributes may affect this process. It is written primarily for those who engage in qualitative research with children in particular, and qualitative researchers in general. It should also be of interest to individuals interested in gender issues, education, and cross-cultural research.

Throughout the text, the reader will find numerous citations from works by women anthropologists and the feminist literature. These citations are vital to accomplish the goals of the text, and appear in part because: a) I am a female researcher, and this book is in part about how a researcher's gender affects the fieldwork process with children; and b) most publications generated on gender issues and the subjective aspects of fieldwork are undertaken by women social scientists (see the exceptional works by Abramson, 1993; Back, 1993; Kulick & Wilson, 1995; McKeganey & Bloor, 1991; Wade, 1993, for contributions by male researchers). The male perspective is covered differentially partly due to the paucity of literature, and examples are drawn from my experiences as a female fieldworker.

The intention of this work is to encourage those who conduct fieldwork with children (and adults) to consider the influence that factors such as gender and ethnicity have on this process. It should not be viewed as the definitive source on this topic. Rather, I hope it is received as a preliminary work that stimulates dialogue between fieldworkers on issues that are relatively unexplored in conducting fieldwork with children.

I focus on methodological issues, data collection and analysis, and the interpretation of children's cultures. Further, I view fieldwork and establishing field relationships as bidirectional processes (Maccoby, 1992). For example, certain factors and personal characteristics of the fieldworker affect his or her interactions with children. Children are active actors in field relationships, and their behavior mutually affects the fieldworker's interactions with them. The acknowledgment of such influences and factors during the fieldwork process should (I hope) enrich ethnographic interpretations and the written work.

Finally, other factors or personal attributes of the researcher may also affect the fieldwork process. These include but are not limited to: a) age (Thorne, 1993); b) social and marital status (e.g., Beoku-Betts, 1994); c) physical appearance (e.g., McKeganey & Bloor, 1991); d) research orientation (Clifford, 1983; Sutton-Smith, 1994); and e) theoretical perspectives and political agendas (Van Maanen, 1988). Although these factors are important and deserve attention, they are not discussed here. I readily acknowledge that gender, ethnicity, age, and social status are often entwined and act in concert as they influence field relationships and ethnographic interpretations. In this work, gender and ethnicity are discussed as distinct attributes.

The material that follows is supported by examples extracted from my field experiences with children on school premises over the past 12 years. Chapter 2, "Methods: Working With Children," provides a discussion on methods that includes access to school field sites; establishing relationships with the children; interviewing children; and ethical concerns. Practical strategies for working with children are offered. In Chapter 3, "School Organization and Culture," the reader is introduced to schooling, school personnel and gender, and fieldworker interactions with school personnel. This chapter also contains material on cross-cultural early childhood educational experiences. Chapter 4, "Fieldwork and Gender," examines the link between conducting fieldwork with children and the researcher's gender. This chapter contains discussions on how the fieldworker's gender affects the choice of methods, data collection, and ethnographic interpretation. Topics addressed include sex differences, interviewing children, data collection and observation, and interpretations of children's cultures. Chapter 5, "Fieldwork and Ethnicity," explores the effect of a fieldworker's ethnicity on the fieldwork process. Topics discussed include the influence of cultural ideals and values on the interpretation of children's cultures and cross-cultural views of childhood. Chapter 6, "Concluding Remarks," contains a summary of the ideas and findings presented and practical suggestions for conducting fieldwork with children.

CHAPTER 2

Methods: Working With Children

The intention of this chapter is not to reiterate the guidelines that exist on how to conduct fieldwork with children, such as what role to adopt, learning about children's cultures, and how and what to observe. This is accomplished succinctly by Fine and Sandstrom (1988) and Pellegrini (1996). Rather, this chapter contains traditional methodological concerns and some practical strategies for working with children. These include: a) access to the field site and subsequent access to all members of the culture; b) establishing rapport with the children; c) interviewing children; and d) ethical concerns.

In addition, I explore how a researcher's gender and ethnicity can affect some aspects of the fieldwork process with children. The importance of a fieldworker's personal attributes in guiding the fieldwork experience is rarely recognized or discussed in ethnographic works on children.

The material that follows is based on my field experiences with children over the past decade. I have primarily conducted fieldwork in elementary schools with kindergarten children. On occasion, I have engaged in fieldwork in nursery schools and day care centers. Additionally, I've conducted quantitative studies with children who ranged in age from 5 to 11 years old.

Most of my field studies are year-long commitments. The research questions I tend to pursue are best served by extended stays with the children. Sometimes, I have simultaneously engaged in two projects. In these instances, one is always short-term; the other is a year-long commitment. In the latter projects, I typically enter the field on the first day of class and depart at the end of the school year. During my fieldwork, I have explored topics such as children's play, ethnic beliefs, social distance, and friendship.

Over the years, I have conducted fieldwork in approximately 20 schools. I have visited about 12 more for various reasons such as school-related duties (e.g., observing students at field sites), invitations to school functions, and family matters. I have conducted fieldwork in schools that are racially segregated (with both majority and minority populations) and racially mixed. I have worked in lower-income, disadvantaged schools where some children are homeless, and in middle- to upper-middle-income schools where some children are privileged. The former usually have a higher percentage of minority children; the latter usually have a higher percentage of majority children. In each school, I employed the same strategy to seek permission to conduct my research and adopted the same researcher role with the children.

Access to Field Sites

Acquiring permission to conduct fieldwork with children on school premises is an arduous and time-consuming task. Schools are often reluctant to grant permission for a variety of reasons that include past experiences with other researchers, concern for the children's well-being, happenings in the community, and the nature or topic of the project (see also Graue & Walsh, in press).

I consistently employ the same strategy when requesting permission to visit with the children. First, I contact the principal of the school (or director of the nursery school or day care center) to see if my visit will be agreeable with him or her. If the principal is comfortable with the proposal, I submit a letter of explanation to the board of education.

The letter of explanation varies depending on the project. For most of my fieldwork studies, I submit a letter that includes a detailed explanation of the project, when and how often I wish to visit the children, my school affiliation and credentials, and a discussion of ethical concerns. The latter includes an agreement to protect the children and the school's privacy. I emphasize the following provisions: I promise to use pseudonyms for the children and school in any resulting publications, and I will neither photograph nor videotape the children. Typically, the research proposal is presented and either passed or rejected as a motion at a board of education meeting. Once accepted, my school placement is then arranged. I customarily arrange an appointment to meet with the principal and the host teacher to discuss the project.

Fieldworkers working with children in schools must confront the notion that the children rarely, if ever, are responsible for giving their own consent to participate. Rather, consent is obtained from either the board of education or parents. This is due in part to the fact that children are minors (Fine & Sandstrom, 1988; see the related works by Hall & Lin, 1995, and Wescott, 1994, for ethical concerns regarding child witnesses and children's mental health treatments).

For example, I have not had to obtain individual parental consent for any study I have conducted on school premises. The board of education acted on the children's behalf and granted permission for my projects in part because the studies have been observational studies and I promised to protect the children and the school's identity. Experimental manipulation, diagnostic testing, or studies that require access to the children's records are more difficult to pursue and have accepted because such designs require parental consent and may disrupt the children's daily routines.

In reality and unlike adults, children have very few rights as participants. In agreement with Fine and Sandstrom (1988), I have always supplied the children with an explanation about my projects that is developmentally appropriate. On the first day of class, I invite the children to sit on the floor with me in a circle. At this time, I explain the project to them. I answer any questions they may have about the project or my presence in their class. I tell them that there are no right or wrong answers to any of the questions I may ask them, and that they do not have to participate in activities if they do not wish to. Some children find it hard to believe that a grown-up actually wants to go to school with them and learn about things such as play or friendship. I suspect that for children, school is a place where children go, whereas grown-ups go off to work. Most children accept my explanation of the project and my presence, and most never give it any thought after that.

Establishing Rapport With the Children

The most important ingredient in conducting fieldwork with young children is the desire to work with them (Fine & Sandstrom, 1988). A researcher working with children should possess the following personality characteristics and qualities. He or she should: a) be patient; b) have no qualms about acting "silly" according to some adult standards of the term; c) be prepared to experience manipulation and domination by children willingly, particularly at playtime (e.g., Fine, 1987; Fine & Sandstrom, 1988; Kelly-Byrne, 1989; Mandell, 1988); d) be competent in matters of child development; and e) be willing to accept the candor of young children (Holmes, 1995).

Not one of these conditions is related remotely to or influenced by a researcher's gender. Male and female fieldworkers alike may possess these characteristics and qualities. In addition, most male and female fieldworkers who engage in participant observation with children adopt the "friend role" (Fine & Sandstrom, 1988; Mandell, 1988). Mandell (1988) defines the "least adult role" in studying children as one in which the fieldworker exerts no authority over the children and establishes a trusting relationship that is modeled after the friendship bond. The key ingredients necessary to achieve the friend role are expressing positive feelings and a desire to be with the children, the failure to deliver discipline, and treating the children with respect (Fine & Sandstrom, 1988).

Such a role allows the researcher to gain the children's trust and attenuate the researcher's authority that is implied inherently in the social status of grown-up. It is the role I employ when working with children of all ages, and I believe this role is partly responsible for the ease with which I am able to gain and earn children's trust.

For example, I believe the following actions have helped me establish rapport with the children. First, where feasible I ask for a bus assignment so that I can ride with some of the children to school. The bus is a great place to establish relationships, particularly because there is minimal adult interference. Second, I request that the teachers treat me like a student. I do schoolwork with the kids, have snack with them, take part in physical education classes, go on school trips, and receive discipline from the teachers for any wrongdoing on my part (time-out can be a killer, even for 5 minutes). I turn in homework and try to behave in ways far removed from the other adults in the school.

Third, I always use the children's equipment (e.g., crayons, pencils, paints). For example, I sit in their scaled-down chairs even though the adult chairs are far more comfortable. Fourth, I always interact with the children at their eye level. Thus, I spend a great deal of time bending, kneeling, and sitting on the floor when I interact with them. I have never addressed a child while he or she was seated and I was standing. This only serves to reinforce what children already know—that grown-ups have power over them.

Finally, I attempt to learn the children's culturally approved responses for child-child and child-teacher interactions as quickly as possible. This includes learning how to ask to join a play group, how to respond to a teacher's request, and how to play a variety of games and activities. This behavioral repertoire is as crucial as sharing and cooperation. It is also no secret that children enjoy being with people who enjoy being with them.

For young children, play and friendship are entwined, and becoming a competent player helps me establish and maintain friendships with the children. It's a great way to build rapport with them. Being invited to the children's birthdays and not being identified or labeled *teacher* by them are clear signs that I have established a rapport with the children and earned their trust.

Although it is possible for adult fieldworkers to participate in children's cultures, I do acknowledge that the salient differences between children and adults (e.g., physical size and power) can never completely be eliminated. Adult fieldworkers are never fully accepted into children's cultures because they can never relinquish their adult status. Rather, the fieldworker becomes the learner and the children become the teachers in the fieldworker's attempt to experience the children's ways of knowing about the world.

There have been times when the children have manipulated our friendship bond (see also Kelly-Byrne, 1989). Several children have attempted to use our friendship bond (e.g., threatening to dissolve it) to coerce me into doing their homework for them. I always met this request with a negative response, and countered the request with asking them to help me with my homework. My refusal to help did not appear to affect our friendship, because these children and I remained friends even after I refused to help them. I believe they were merely testing the boundaries of our relationship.

I was also coerced into playing games in which I did not wish to participate (although I always did, and with zeal, I might add). This usually occurred when I was trying to observe other activities or was already playing in an established play group. I was also assigned frequently the role of "it" and "the chaser" (in games of chase), "pitcher," and "big sister" (even though I preferred other play roles). In addition, I always let the children lead in play (unless of course I was the play group boss) and never coerced them into playing something I wanted to play. Most of the time, the children controlled and dictated my play behavior.

This addresses the recent concern of postmodern social scientists regarding the nature of the researcher-subject relationship (e.g., Clifford, 1988; Van Maanen, 1988, 1995). Adult-child relationships are distinct and lopsided because of gaps in age, physical size, and possession of power. I knew that the children would respond positively to most of my requests because young children typically seek adult approval. I didn't want the children to feel pressured to converse with me. So I let them approach me first, and when I thought they were comfortable with me, I began to ask questions. I prefaced requests for help with phrases such as, "If you're not busy playing right now ... " or simply conversed with the kids while we were playing.

I was frequently dominated and manipulated by the children (see also Kelly-Byrne's, 1989, ethnography for a discussion of her experiences playing regularly with one child), however. For me, this illustrates the importance of acknowledging contextual information when interpreting the children's behavioral and social interactions. To borrow Rosaldo's (1989) notion of "positioned subjects," and depending on my contextual interactions with the children, there was an imbalance of power in my field relationships with them. This scale was tipped frequently in the children's favor. This statement requires an explanation.

First, my grown-up status was presumably very attenuated in the classroom. I explained to the teachers that I needed to relinquish my grown-up status so the children would view me as much as possible as a student. To accomplish this, the teachers treated me as much as possible like a student. Second, I adopted the friend role during fieldwork. The children knew I neither disciplined them nor represented a real authority figure. The only time I did intervene was when children were involved in a physical fight or if I thought the children could be physically harmed if I did not take action (see also Fine & Sandstrom, 1988). I also believe the children were aware that I possessed dual social status—namely, student and grown-up. Some of the children were clever in this respect, and negotiated the social status that would best help them accomplish their goals.

Other children tried (and some succeeded) to get me in trouble with the teacher. For example, some children intentionally placed me in compromising situations. In one instance, Todd asked me to retrieve some items (toys that the children brought from home that the school did not condone) from a storage shelf. Because I typically visited the children once a week, I relied on them to teach me the class rules. This also helped me establish a rapport with them. I was unaware that the items he requested were prohibited in the classroom and proceeded to get them (I should have known by his wide grin that this was not a good idea). The teacher informed me that children were never supposed to touch these items. I was then asked to reveal the name of the child who sent me to get the items. I knew that the popular children did not tattle and that friends do not tell on one another. I simply replied that I had gotten the items on my own. This earned me a time-out for 5 minutes during free play. My failure to tell on Todd strengthened the rapport I had already established with him, and we became great friends. I learned and employed the rules of friendship, how these influenced their (and my) play behavior, and how friendship bonds could be maintained, manipulated, and bartered to meet one's needs.

At times, it appeared as though the children dictated and controlled the direction my research project was taking. Sometimes, I wanted to observe an activity of interest passively but this was next to impossible. The children were demanding of my time, pulled me into play when I was observing, and interrupted me when I was trying to jot down notes. I learned to move with the children's rhythms, to take notes while playing, and to employ culturally acceptable responses to the children's requests. The latter proved to be quite fruitful. For example, when children tire of one play activity, they frequently walk away without verbal warning from the individual or group with whom they are playing. I employed this strategy when I needed to exit a play group or leave a demanding child behind, or wanted to observe another activity.

Interviewing Children

A generous amount of literature has been produced on the problems associated with interviewing children, particularly children who are victims of sexual abuse (e.g., Faller & Everson, 1996; Greenstock & Pipe, 1996; Steward, Bussey, Goodman, & Saywitz, 1993). Interviewing children in the field is particularly problematic on school premises for several reasons. First, although you have several windows of opportunity during free play (this time is the most productive), the noise level is typically loud and the background noise is disruptive. A tape recorder is useless during playtime. I use it either to substantiate my field notes or when I can talk to the children during quiet time. And just when you're deeply involved in a good interview session, a child may decide spontaneously to get up and join a play group he or she sees nearby. Other times, several children will intrude on your conversation.

Thus, male and female fieldworkers have to devise strategies that are fruitful for the children with whom and the classroom circumstance in which they're working. For example, occasionally during free play I have donned a hat and asked the children to play newspaper reporter with me. This was productive because the children seemed willing to play, and I was able to interview them informally, individually, and in small groups. The game often lasted for a while. We alternated roles, and the children had the opportunity to interview me and take notes while I was talking. This was a good strategy because some children could not understand why or what I was always writing in my notebook (even though I repeatedly told them). They often imitated me while we played this game, and it gave both of us the opportunity to engage in role reversal.

An issue in interviewing children is how one phrases a query. Elizabeth Loftus (1975, 1991; see also Loftus & Zanni, 1975) has written extensively on eyewitness testimony and how the phrasing of questions can influence memory of an event. The key is to avoid misleading questions or getting the children to say what you want to hear (e.g., Greenstock & Pipe, 1996). To circumvent these problems, I phrase a question in several different ways, and try to give all the children the same questions phrased in similar ways (Holmes, 1992). Additionally, it is important to make the queries developmentally appropriate. Language competency varies greatly among children, and I try to tailor my questions and conversations around the child's language abilities.

I neither conduct structured interviews with the children nor intentionally take them out of their classroom for the purpose of interviewing them. The latter situation is anxiety producing for them, and the children equate being separated from their classmates with the notion that they have misbehaved in some way. I find that informal or unstructured interviewing (during free play in the classroom, on the playground, on the bus, etc.) works best, and I have integrated asking children to draw for me while I am talking with them. This strategy seems to be successful. Most children love to draw, and when they do they tend to concentrate on their drawing. Thus, they are able to answer questions without being distracted, and often will choose to finish their creation before they join another play group (Holmes, 1995). One technical point: I tend to interview the children at their eye level (e.g., while both of us are seated or with me bending down when the child is standing).

Interviewing children can be facilitated by taking into account the child's ethnicity. For example, African American children are socialized to be more people-oriented and tend to perform better in small cooperative groups than European American children (e.g., Hale, 1986). African American children seem to enjoy the group setting. The children can sustain conversation for longer periods of time, they get a chance to interact with one another, and shyer children are more inclined to participate when I interview them as a group. You have to guide the children's narratives into the directions you wish to pursue. Otherwise you tend to collect numerous personal anecdotes with no connecting theme. I use informal interviewing with individual children either when we are playing or when I ask them to draw for me. Both scenarios are productive.

By contrast, European American children are socialized to be more individualistic and independent than African American children (e.g., Hale, 1986). I find that European American children are easier to interview individually as opposed to in a group setting. Thus, fieldworkers working with children might consider the compatibility between interview techniques and a child's ethnicity.

Ethical Concerns

All researchers, by virtue of a personal and professional code of ethics, are painfully aware of the need to protect the rights of their participants. This is a paramount concern for researchers who conduct fieldwork with minors (e.g., Fine & Sandstrom, 1988; Sieber & Sieber, 1992). Earlier in this chapter, I mentioned issues related to ethical concerns when working with children. The first is the knowledge that children as participants have few rights accorded to them, and most often consent for their participation is given by adults such as members of a school board or parents.

Second, all fieldworkers promise to protect their participants from undue stress and harm. With children, special concerns for their well-being include any physical, psychological, or emotional injury that might occur during the field visit. Such injury may occur on school premises or be inflicted by external sources. I discipline children only when I believe my failure to do so will result in a child being physically injured. The fieldworker in schools may be confronted with situations where physical or psychological injury is sustained in other environments, however. Thus, fieldworkers working with minors in schools need to be prepared to deal with a variety of situations that can be potentially threatening to a child's well-being, and should be trained in the proper courses of action to take in such circumstances.

One of these circumstances is suspicion of possible child abuse. Over the years, I have noticed suspicious bruises on two children, and immediately reported them to the teacher. In the states in which I've conducted fieldwork, teachers are required by law to report such an incident. Thus, I knew that alerting the teacher to the bruises would result in her following the proper legal procedures for reporting such suspicions. In each case, I noticed the bruises while the child was hanging upside down on the jungle gym. I find that typical and unusual bruises on the children are revealed during physical education class and outdoor play in warmer weather because the children are inclined to wear light and looser fitting clothing.

Threats to a child's psychological, emotional, and physical well-being may also be revealed to the fieldworker in his or her private conversations with children. Kevin was a sweet, friendly, and good-natured child, and we quickly became friends. Over the course of a few months, however, I noticed a change in his demeanor and behavior.

Although he remained good-natured, he became especially pensive. One day when he and I were playing alone in the sandbox, he said, "Can I tell you something? I hate my life. I just want to kill myself." This statement, coupled with his change in behavior, was extremely disturbing. I spoke to his teacher immediately after class and repeated the conversation Kevin and I had. The matter was attended to with concern and urgency. It also was handled in such a way that Kevin did not know I had revealed our private conversation to the teacher.

Third, there is the legitimate concern that school personnel may be the target of child molestation accusations. In every school I have visited, I was cautioned by either the principal or the head teacher not to engage in any type of physical contact with the children. I was told never to place myself in a situation where I was alone in a room with a child or give first aid to any child who needed it. I abided by the school rules aware of the legal issues that could be raised if I had any interactions with the children in which we were physically close. I confess that it was very difficult for me not to be affectionate with the children. On occasion, I couldn't resist tousling their hair, returning a tickle when they tickled me, or putting an arm around their shoulder when they came to me seeking comfort.

As England (1994) notes, fieldwork is personal, and in conducting fieldwork with children, I have found it difficult to divide my professional (objective) and personal (subjective) actions. The theoretical separation of self from other is not so easily accomplished in fieldwork with children. As Back (1993) notes, the boundaries between the self and the other become redefined and obscured during fieldwork, and I have struggled with how to maintain this distinction. I settled on a position with which I was (and am) comfortable—"self as other." Hence, I have often displayed my affection for the children through physical actions such as tousling their hair, holding their hands, and returning a hug.

Once I was informed about the school's position on physical contact with the children and its legal implications, the subject was never mentioned again. I found this unusual because on more than one occasion such as class trips, parents saw the children hugging me and never queried the teachers about either my identity or my presence in the classroom. Presumably, they were responding to behavioral and social cues (a European American female, comfortable in a school setting, and the approximate age of the children's parents) and thought I was a teacher, parent, or preservice teacher. With respect to school culture in American society, these were legitimate roles that females fulfill.

Teachers of young children are not usually males (e.g., Cohen, 1990; Kauppinen-Toropainen & Lammi, 1993; Rury, 1989), and male researchers working with young children are a rarity in most schools. Their presence is not explained easily because the majority of American fathers do not visit their children's classrooms when school is in session. This is in contrast to the children's mothers and other females who are visible in the school and volunteer frequently to be teachers' aides and classroom helpers.

It appears as though the gender of the fieldworker may also affect the perceptions of the individuals who are present when he or she interacts with the children. In American culture, we are far less suspicious of unfamiliar female adult-child interactions than we are of unfamiliar male adult-child interactions (Rane & Draper, 1995).[1] In addition, the nurturing qualities attributed to women invite suspicion of molestation and abuse when displayed by men in American society.[2] These qualities enrich the early educational experiences of children, yet it is these qualities that male teachers are fearful of demonstrating because of societal pressures (Allan, 1993; see also McKeganey & Bloor, 1991, for an example of an outsider's perceptions of cross-gender, adult-child field relationships).

Another ethical concern in conducting research with children, particularly with low-income, disadvantaged children (e.g., Scott-Jones, 1994) is the issue of reciprocity. With respect to reciprocity, I occasionally bring the children (as a group) treats and goodies during the year and when my fieldwork ends. I have never given a child a reward or gift for helping me learn about his or her culture (e.g., drawing for me or participating in an informal interview).

When working with children in disadvantaged schools, however, fieldworkers are frequently exposed to and have to confront the harsh realities and environments in which these children live. It is difficult not to acknowledge the disparate childhoods children experience and how powerless children are in the adult world. In these settings, I find it difficult to remain detached during and after the fieldwork period.

In the disadvantaged schools, I have anonymously donated clothes and toys to the children. I have also made requests for clothes donations for impoverished children in my university classes, to which my students have graciously responded. I did not believe I was a lone crusader or that I was performing some extraordinary philanthropic act. I knew that these acts, although important to me, would not lead to any discernible changes in the children's quality of life. Some of the children's teachers performed such acts on a regular basis. The feminist literature appears to be exceptional insofar as it contains publications on how scholars have helped those they study (D. Wolf, 1996b).

For me, the promise to protect the children from harm and ensure their well-being was extended to providing material goods for them. I attributed my behavior directly to the socialization experiences from my microsystem—children should be cared for and protected—and macrosystem—American women are socialized to nurture children.

I do not view my personal involvement in fieldwork as an obstruction to describing and interpreting children's cultures. Rather, I see my actions as adding power to my interpretations of children's cultures because I take into account the whole life experiences of the children and the emotions I experience while conducting fieldwork with them.

Before concluding this chapter, I wish to address briefly the relationship between the children and the researcher's ethnicity. First, one concern of postmodern social scientists involves the researcher-subject relationship. In this regard, most of the children with whom I have conducted research are from African American, European American, and Latino ethnic groups. Thus, there has been a match in ethnicity between me and only some of the children with whom I have worked.

In my work *How Young Children Perceive Race* (1995), I contend that my ethnicity did not affect my ability to interpret the children's experiences. I still believe this to be true for several reasons. First, other researchers have reported that the investigator's ethnicity did not influence the child subjects in their projects (e.g., Clark, Hocevar, & Dembo, 1980; Corenblum & Wilson, 1982). Similar reports appear in research conducted with adult populations (e.g., Berik, 1996). For example, Stack (1996) and Back (1993) were able to circumvent their ethnicity during their fieldwork and establish field relationships in black communities.

Second, I have never experienced a situation where I could not establish rapport with a child because of my ethnicity. I have never had a child refuse to interact with me because I was white or dissimilar to him or her in matters of skin color, heritage, or religious beliefs.[3] Rather, I believe the children judged me according to the roles I established with them (i.e., the friend role), my desire to be with them, how accommodating I was as a playmate, and the fact that, like them, I had to abide by the teacher's rules.

Notes

1. I teach a qualitative methods laboratory course in children's play. In this course, students conduct research in off-campus field sites such as day care centers, nursery schools, and elementary schools. During our visits with the directors or principals, the students were informed about the ethical concerns when working with children. Differential treatment for males and females in places where children gather was reinforced for me during these visits. The male students were especially cautioned because they were young, unfamiliar males and might be perceived as child molesters by parents and other adults in the center.

2. Males do commit an overwhelming number of child molestation instances in the general population, but this pattern does not hold true in child care environments.

3. Young children do not employ the arbitrary and socially constructed terms for ethnic groups employed by social scientists. Thus, young children tend to categorize people on the basis of overt qualities such as skin color or the language one speaks. The children with whom I worked used terms such as *white, brown,* and *black* when identifying individuals or categorizing people into groups (see Holmes, 1995).

CHAPTER 3

School Organization and Culture

Because the majority of fieldwork with children takes place in schools (Goodwin, 1997), the material in this chapter contains information relevant to young children's educational experiences and a fieldworker's interactions in this environment. Topics covered include schooling, how schools are a reflection of cultural values (this resurfaces in Chapter 5, "Fieldwork and Ethnicity," as it relates to the fieldworker's cultural background), school curriculum, school and gender, and peer culture.

Education

For a society to be viable, it must find a way to maintain and transmit its values, beliefs, and ways of knowing to each new generation. Education is one institution that fulfills this function (Spindler & Spindler, 1990); the means by which societies educate their children is culture-specific (Woodill, 1992).

According to Johnson (1985), education is the "systematic transmission and inculcation of social and cultural information" (p. 8). He suggests that education is far more than the acquisition of factual and cultural knowledge. Through this process, an individual acquires a more profound understanding about one's own existence.

Two complementary social and cultural forces are involved in the educational process: a) *socialization*—the process by which one acquires culturally acceptable behavior patterns from parents, teachers, siblings, and others (Ember & Ember, 1988); and b) *enculturation*—the implicit knowledge passed on indirectly through observation and inference that helps younger members learn culturally acceptable behaviors (Segall, Dasen, Berry, & Poortinga, 1990).

Both socialization and enculturation are processes that describe how individuals learn culturally acceptable forms of behavior (Chick & Barnett, 1995). These two processes are not interchangeable, however. Rather, implicit in the socialization process is the notion of social control. For example, consider the socialization processes American children experience in schools. In this setting, the teacher-student and older child-younger child relationship serve as one kind of social control mechanism that shapes children's socialization experiences. By contrast, in enculturation, knowledge is gained primarily through inference and observation rather than by direct teaching from a trained professional. In this process, there is an absence of social control (Segall et al., 1990).

Different methods of teaching have been identified cross-culturally (see Ahmed's, 1983, work on traditional, informal, and formal educational techniques). In this work, I focus on the traditional western method of formal education—schooling.

American life experiences take place for the most part in settings away from the home. For example, most adults spend their waking hours at work, whereas children spend their days at school (Goodman, 1992; Rutter, Maugham, Mortimore, & Ouston, 1979). As Goffman (1961) notes, it is within institutions that individuals function according to a certain set of prescriptions for behavior. One of the more visible institutions in developed countries is the school. In these societies, schools play a vital role in academic instruction and socializing children (Goodman, 1992; Spindler & Spindler, 1990; Tobin, Wu, & Davidson, 1989).

School Culture as a Reflection of a Society's Cultural Ideology

Because fieldwork studies with children in schools have taken place in different countries (e.g., Laing & Pang, 1992; Tobin et al., 1989), I have elected to include cross-cultural philosophies of kindergarten education. The focus is on early childhood education because the majority of my fieldwork has been with kindergarten (and preschool) children.

In the American school system, kindergarten is the beginning of compulsory education.[1] The National Association for the Education of Young Children (NAEYC) has advanced guidelines that emphasize the most effective developmental and individual practices for children for the first 8 years of life (Bredekamp, 1987; see also Bredekamp & Rosegrant, 1992). Although not an exhaustive list, these guidelines emphasize the importance of integrative learning, learning through play and exploration, having children self-select activities from available opportunities, recognizing individual variation in learning and development, and encouraging the teacher to undertake small group and individual instruction rather than whole group instruction (see also Hsue, 1995).

Some contemporary kindergarten curriculum still stresses academic skills and neglects children's total development. Gelb and Bishop (1992) report that most kindergarten lessons today are comparable to lessons taught in the first grade in past decades. The American notion of accelerated academic kindergarten classes does not hold true cross-culturally.

In Argentina, the preschool educational experience of 4- and 5-year-old children is equivalent to the American kindergarten. Argentinean children may attend kindergarten in either half-day or full-day sessions; the latter arose partly as a solution to child care needs for working mothers. In recognition of the importance of preschool education to a child's total development, there is a current movement to integrate preschool education into the national school curriculum rather than have it controlled individually by provinces (Hurtado, 1992).

In Australia, kindergarten and preschool are synonymous with educational experiences that take place prior to mandatory schooling. Children may opt to attend half-day kindergarten sessions 1 to 5 days a week. Parental beliefs about kindergarten focus on its preparatory function for primary school and its socialization benefits. The Australian kindergarten curriculum, like that of Japan and China, emphasizes play as a medium through which children learn. Thus, free play occupies an overwhelming portion of the school day. Other highlights in the Australian curriculum include helping children become self-reliant, promoting language skills and self-expression, and encouraging problem solving. Finally, in contrast to American schools, kindergarten teachers in Australia guide children's learning experiences rather than dictate what activities they should pursue (McLean, Piscitelli,

Halliwell, & Ashby, 1992). This parallels the philosophy of early childhood specialist Maria Montessori.

Other countries also separate kindergarten from the primary schools and compulsory education. In Iran, kindergarten is viewed as preparation for formal schooling. Attendance is not mandatory, and most children who attend do so as a child care arrangement rather than for instruction (Sabbaghian, 1992).

The United States

The culture of a school is a reflection of a society's cultural values and ideology. In addition to imparting academic knowledge, schools (along with parents, relatives, peers, religious institutions, the media, etc.) function as one kind of socializing agent for children (Johnson, 1985; Spindler & Spindler, 1990; Tobin et al., 1989).

American school culture is undoubtedly a reflection of mainstream American culture. In American schools, children learn appropriate American core values such as achievement and being the best, the cultural ideology of individualism (Spence, 1985; Triandis & Berry, 1981), and their position in American society. American schools promote self-discipline and freedom of choice. Schoolchildren learn early on that their achievements will be met with adult approval, and achievement will be gained through self-discipline and hard work (Engel, 1988; Spence, 1985; Spindler & Spindler, 1990).[2] Even the position statement advanced by the NAEYC reflects the core American values of equality, fairness, and justice (Hsue, 1995).

School is one of the places where children learn the culturally appropriate responses adults will expect of them. In addition, school (like the neighborhood) is an environment where children learn and acquire knowledge about their peer culture (e.g., Corsaro & Eder, 1990; Konner, 1991). Such socialization processes begin in preschool, where children learn parental expectations and cultural values such as independence and self-reliance. These values find expression in preschool curriculums that allow children the freedom to select their own activities and search for self-expression.

Japan

The global trend of increasing numbers of women entering the workforce has affected preschool education cross-culturally (Woodill, Bernhard, & Prochner, 1992). Preschools are becoming popular in countries all over the world partly because they are a solution to the problem of child care.

In Japan, preschool education takes place at two distinct institutions—the *yochien* and the *hoikuen*. The final year of the *yochien* and *hoikuen* is equivalent to the American kindergarten experience. The distinction between the *yochien* and *hoikuen* parallels the differentiation made between nursery schools and day care centers in the United States (Tobin et al., 1989). The *yochien* includes children from the ages of 3 to 6 years, whereas the *hoikuen* accepts children from 6 months until 6 years.

Additionally, in contrast to American educational pedagogy, kindergartens in Japan are not part of the primary school experience. Compulsory schooling starts after the 6th birthday and continues for 9 years (Tabu & Aoki, 1990). Tabu and Aoki (1990) compiled a comprehensive review and description of early childhood education in Japan. The following summary is extracted from that work.

Japanese children between the ages of 3 and 6 years are eligible to attend kindergarten any time during this period. School meets 220 days of the year, 4 hours a day. A typical day in a Japanese kindergarten begins when the children enter the school, greet their teacher, put away their belongings, and have a few minutes to socialize before class begins. This is analogous to the morning routine in an American kindergarten.

What differs between American and Japanese kindergartens is the percentage of time devoted to particular tasks. For example, in Japanese kindergartens, play occupies a central focus in the curriculum. Play is used as a medium through which children are taught factual knowledge, social skills, and group values. In fact, part of the teacher's role is to select developmentally appropriate and stimulating play activities. The teacher introduces new play activities to the children when he or she senses inattentiveness or the onset of boredom. Children spend most of their morning engaged in play activities, and then break for lunch. After lunch, the children rest and engage in quiet activities such as reading books and making puzzles and origami. During the school day, emphasis is placed on encouraging group interaction (e.g., Tobin et al., 1989).

This stands in contrast to American kindergartens. In 1987, NAEYC advanced a position document that contains the best educational practices for children from birth through age 8 (Bredekamp, 1987; see also Bredekamp & Rosegrant, 1992). This statement was generated in response to earlier programs that emphasized teacher-directed instruction and academic skills training (Schickedanz, 1994). In an effective kindergarten classroom, one should be able to observe children playing and working with peers, a varied selection of materials, minimal whole group instruction, children's artwork, learning experiences integrated into the children's life experiences, abundant playtime, infrequent completion of worksheets, and a curriculum that accommodates interindividual variation in learning ("Top 10 signs," 1996).

In my fieldwork experiences in kindergarten classrooms, classroom practice has not always kept pace with the curriculum guidelines established by NAEYC. I have experienced polar extremes in classroom practice. Several exceptional classrooms met and exceeded NAEYC's guidelines for appropriate practice. Several teachers frequently used small cooperative group arrangements and integrated classroom learning with the children's life experiences, encouraged child exploration, and employed emergent curriculums. Worksheets in these classrooms occupied only a small percentage of the day. In other schools, little had changed in the children's daily routines over the past decade. A good majority of the classrooms were academically oriented, and the children spent a large part of their day in whole group instruction (Day, 1988; Gelb & Bishop, 1992).

In the kindergarten classes I have visited, each possessed a similar curriculum. Although individual teachers tried to integrate innovative teaching techniques and themes in their classrooms, most followed a common routine. In the morning, children entered the classroom, greeted the teacher, put away their belongings, and engaged in a few minutes of free play. Then the day's class routine began. A typical kindergarten day was often compartmentalized, with specific periods of time devoted to the alphabet, math concepts, arts and crafts, reading, free play, and physical education. As Bredekamp (1987) suggests, this constrained approach is due in part to the teacher's sense of urgency to "cover the curriculum" (p. 63). Many teachers express frustration over their desire to move away from traditional worksheets to small group cooperative learning and child-initiated activities. Their desire is displaced by the fact that they have to adhere to the school's curriculum, however. In fact, their continuance in the school depends on it.

Special activities such as developmental education and library typically occurred once a week on the same day and at the same time of day. Computer class also occurred once a week in schools that possessed the necessary resources. Disadvantaged schools typically had one computer in the classroom, which the children shared. In some of the classrooms, small cooperative group learning was rarely practiced. Rather, the kids spent a large part of their day involved in teacher-led projects that were completed individually. Periods of instruction ranged from approximately 15 to 25 minutes. Some teachers expected all the children to finish at the same time and paid no attention to individual differences. Slower children had to sit and finish their work while other children were allowed to move on to other activities. Some especially slow children were asked to take unfinished class work home and complete it for homework. Two schools had no outdoor play period for kindergarten children.

On the brighter side, all the classrooms possessed a diverse assortment of play materials, an indoor play period, a class pet, displays of the children's creations, and encouraged social interaction between children. Every teacher encouraged self-exploration in her students and tried to incorporate experiential kinds of learning assignments into the children's day.

In contrast to Japanese preschools, play in some American kindergartens occupies only a peripheral position and takes place at designated times during the school day, if at all. Many early childhood educators have argued that American children receive academic skills training at too early an age and at the expense of their total development (e.g., Day, 1988; Egertson, 1987; Elkind, 1981; Zigler, 1987). This may be due in part to the place of kindergarten in the American system. Some researchers view this grade as belonging to early childhood; other researchers align it with first grade.

In addition, American educational pedagogy reflects the cultural values of individual achievement, competition, and self-reliance. By contrast, Japanese educational philosophy for kindergartners includes comprehensive guidance and instruction through play (Tabu & Aoki, 1990).

Similar to American kindergartens, Japanese preschools and kindergartens are a reflection of Japan's cultural ideology. Children learn to internalize acceptable cultural norms of behavior in these environments. For example, a "good child"—*Ii ko*—is described as *otonashii* (gentle) and *sunao* (cooperative, compliant, and obedient; Tabu & Aoki, 1990, p. 56). Support emerges from observational studies conducted in various Japanese classrooms. The personality characteristic *sunao* is considered highly desirable by both parents and Japanese society.

Parents know that this quality will help their children become competent adults, and cooperativeness is highly valued in this collectivist, group-oriented society (see also Taylor et al., 1994; White & LeVine, 1986). The parents and teachers interviewed viewed *sunao* as a valued personal quality that allows children to maintain interpersonal harmony within the context of the group. This ability is the cornerstone of Japanese cultural values, and is reflected in the children's school activities.

The collectivist ideology of Japan (e.g., Triandis, 1989; Triandis, Brislin, & Hui, 1988) is strongly reflected in its preschools. In kindergarten, children spend most of their day involved in group play or group projects. Emphasis is placed on finding and sustaining the balance between expressing one's individuality and functioning within the group—between *giri* (obligation) and *ninjo* (human feeling; Tobin et al., 1989, p. 71). After visiting a traditional Japanese kindergarten, Taylor et al. (1994) report that a considerable amount of time is dedicated to group work. Sometimes, the children act in such unison that individual children are hardly recognized. The children appear to function as a single unit.

In their cross-cultural study of preschools, Tobin et al. (1989) note that one function of these institutions is to transmit core cultural and social values to the children who attend them. Thus, Japanese preschools and kindergartens attempt to socialize children to be obedient, gentle, and group oriented and to put forth their best effort. This is accomplished through classroom management techniques that emphasize child-child interactions rather than teacher-child interactions. In their interactions with peers, children learn self-discipline and how to maintain their individuality in a group-oriented society.

China

In Chinese kindergartens, children learn early on that they are members of a collectivist culture (Triandis, 1989; Triandis et al., 1988). Class activities primarily stress group rather than individual activities, and it is not uncommon for children to engage in group-oriented activities for most of the school day (Laing & Pang, 1992). Certain aspects of a collectivist ideology may vary from culture to culture, however.

For example, there are important differences between Japanese and Chinese collectivism. In Chinese collectivism, emphasis is placed on order, and this order must be maintained. This stands in contrast to Japanese collectivism, in which order often appears nonexistent. Rather, it appears as if chaos prevails. This view is reflected in classroom practices. In China, children sit quietly at their desks, and the noise level is typically low during class time. Even lunchtime is a quiet, orderly event, and little socialization occurs between children. By contrast, in Japan, classroom noise levels tend to be high, and it is not uncommon to find children out of their seats exploring their environment (Tobin et al., 1989).

This emphasis on order also surfaces in classroom activities. Tobin et al. (1989) describe an activity in which the children build a block structure from a blueprint of the design. The importance of the task is to teach children how to follow a sequence while maintaining order. Although the children individually are responsible for their own buildings, the task is undertaken within a group context. Emphasis on the importance of the group in Chinese society is extended to daily class rituals such as visiting the lavatories. This is performed as a group so that the children learn to coordinate their body rhythms with those around them.

In line with Japanese thinking on the function of kindergartens, Chinese schools emphasize the moral education of the child (Dahawy, 1993). Chinese children are socialized to internalize the values of their culture, which include love of country and family, orientation to the group, and egalitarianism, such as treating one another equally and with respect (Laing & Pang, 1992; Tobin et al., 1989).

In addition, Chinese kindergarten teachers employ several different methods through which they teach young children. These include play, work, and mundane activities. Play is believed to help children acquire the concept of numbers and to facilitate language development. Work is viewed as a medium through which children become independent while recognizing the importance of the group (Laing & Pang, 1992). Finally, a majority of Chinese kindergartens employ an "on-duty system" that teaches children the importance of personal responsibility and obligation—cultural values considered respectable qualities in children (Laing & Pang, 1992, p. 174).

School Personnel

Researcher Interactions With School Personnel

My interactions with principals over the years have varied from no contact to frequent contact. Meeting with the principal is the first step in entering the field. In all cases, I asked principals to address me by my first name, although I continued to address them by a title followed by their surname. I adopted this strategy for a variety of reasons. First, principals and teachers address children by their first names, whereas children are required to address their teachers and principal by title and surname. I wanted to be treated like a student, and I believed this would help my classmates respond to and accept me as a peer.

All the principals complied with my request when I was with the children or school personnel. When the principals introduced me to unfamiliar school personnel, however, they always did so by my title and surname. There was one exception. One male principal addressed me as either "Miss" followed by my surname or did not use a term of address at all. Most of the time he referred to me as a preservice teacher, although my letter of explanation, which he read, contained my academic credentials and institutional affiliation. It was the only time that I experienced what Johnson (1985) refers to as *male hegemony*.

I would like to address my field relationships with my host teachers. As Williams (1993) contends, teaching is a female-dominated vocation, and all the teachers with whom I worked are female. Every teacher was accommodating and gracious in every possible way, and each made me feel quite comfortable in her class. My gender, vocational choice, age, and shared experiences all served in some way to influence how we constructed our field relationships.

Because I was a female professor and researcher, I believe I was able to identify with the teachers and their teaching experiences in some way. I neither experienced nor perceived an imbalance of power in our relationships. All the teachers were confident and educated women, and they never alluded to differences in our status because I taught at a postsecondary institution. They were supportive of my work, and we occasionally discussed our educational philosophies and classroom experiences. Similarly, it may be easier for male fieldworkers to establish relationships with male administrators and male teachers because they share gender membership and similar experiences.

Forming cross-sex field relationships differs from establishing same-sex relationships insofar as the former carries its own set of prescriptive rules. Establishing cross-sex field relationships may be difficult in some instances because they often imply sexual connotations. They may be difficult to maintain due to a variety of factors that include pressure from community members (e.g., Back, 1993). In my field experiences, establishing cross-sex field relationships with the teachers is a moot point because I never came into contact with a male kindergarten teacher.

School Personnel and Gender

A division of labor by sex is evident in education. Historically, males have occupied positions of power in building and school administration, curriculum development, and educational research. In contrast, women have tended to fill the classrooms, where they implement the curriculums and practices designed by men (Allan, 1993; Kauppinen-Toropainen & Lammi, 1993; Goodman, 1992; Williams, 1995).

Since 1860, women in American society have outnumbered men in the teaching vocation (Allan, 1993; Clifford, 1989). Throughout American history, teachers have been perceived as middle-class females, and by 1930, the occupation of teacher was synonymous with "women's work" (Rury, 1989).

Perceptions of teachers have changed little. In 1962, Margaret Mead gave a lecture on the school in American culture. At this time, a school teacher was perceived to be a middle-class female in her mid-30s who taught the younger primary grades. By the 1980s, teaching had become a voluntary vocational choice. Although civil rights produced an increase in minority teachers, today there is still a disproportionate number of European American, middle-class women in teaching (Allan, 1993; Rury, 1989).

School Culture

Although school culture reflects a society's cultural values, within American schools there exists a separate and distinct culture apart from the larger society. Deal and Peterson (1990) define school culture as the character of the school as it is reflected in the values, beliefs, traditions, and customs formed over time. Cultural values and practices that surface in schools include the rules of interaction in social and formal relationships.

Many researchers have produced ethnographies from field-work conducted in schools. For example, there is Coleman's (1961) work about adolescent society, Corsaro's (1985) study about peer culture in a nursery school, Holmes' (1995) investigation of racial beliefs, Johnson's (1985) work about elementary schools, Schofield's (1981, 1989) studies about racial relations in school, Spindler and Spindler's (1990) work on American education, Rizzo's (1989) work on children's friendships, and Thorne's (1993) work on gender play.

Students initiated into school culture for the most part find themselves seated at individual desks in traditional vertical rows, completing worksheets and receiving instruction from their teacher as a group (Goodlad, 1984; Goodman, 1992). As Tobin et al. (1989) note, schools are a reflection of and socializing agent for cultural values. Thus, American children learn early on that they reside in an individualistic society. Their achievements and failures rest on their own efforts, hard work, and self-discipline—values that are reinforced in American schools.

One of the most important things about school culture that children learn early on is that school is a reflection of the adult world—it is one more domain where adults exert control over them (Goodman, 1992; Maccoby, 1992). Children also come to learn that the power embedded in relationships is not confined to relationships between adults and children. Child-child relationships also possess this ingredient.

At school, relationships between children and adults are often characterized by their formality (Deal & Peterson, 1990; Gee, 1989; Lesko, 1988). This is supported by the terms of address used by both children and adults in the school. When interacting with children, teachers employ children's first names. (Although rare, some teachers use Miss or Mister followed by the child's surname. This presumably signals to the child that disciplinary measures are close at hand.)

When a child addresses a teacher, the child always uses a title (Dr., Mr., Mrs., or Miss) followed by the teacher's surname.

Fieldworkers working with children are quick to note the power implied in child-adult relationships. Thus, fieldworkers often adopt the friend role and request that the children address them by their first name to attenuate their adult authority (see Corsaro, 1985; Fine, 1987; Holmes, 1995). As Goodman (1992) notes, the traditional power frameworks in schools separate and exaggerate the distance between children and adults. For the most part, the prescribed nature of adult-child relationships tends to project the image that adults in school are unapproachable (see also Bryan, 1975).

I recall one incident when a second grader paused on a stairwell to give me the right of way. I suspect his behavior was guided by his perception and classification of me as a grown-up, in part because I was an unfamiliar adult. I gestured for him to go ahead of me, and he gave me a puzzled look followed by "Thank you." His response conveyed a salient message—adults possess the power in schools, and children should defer to adult authority.

Finally, although student-teacher relationships become increasingly formal from early to middle childhood, teachers in the early grades do (in my experience) provide nurturing and caring behaviors for their students (see also Granucci, 1990; Johnson, 1985). Thus, in certain contexts and circumstances, the formal nature of the student-teacher relationship is relaxed (e.g., when a child is injured).

One of the factors responsible for the recent lack of display of physical affection by teachers toward young students is the realistic threat of child molestation accusations. This is particularly true for male teachers. One underlying concern in all the schools I have visited is protecting the children. Only a few decades ago, children walked home from school unescorted, and parents were confident that no misfortune would happen to their children during the school day. Now school doors are locked during school hours to prevent intruders from gaining access to the children, and visitors are required to wear passes that identify them to school personnel. Teachers are cautioned about the distinction between displaying physical affection for children and the potential threat that a teacher's behavior may be perceived as child molestation. Parents also recognize the need to protect their children. They now meet their children at the bus stop rather than allowing them to walk home unescorted by an adult. Such changes reflect the current climate of how American society views children, and the adaptive nature of culture.

Herein lies a major disservice done to children by the very system designed to protect them, however. At a time when young children need nurturance and affection, school culture dictates that teachers should be wary about displaying those behaviors. Children learn more effectively in warm and caring environments, yet the school, in an effort to protect them, strips the children from these rewarding compassionate adult-child relationships. This is not a cross-cultural phenomenon, and in other cultures, young children are not stripped of adult nurturance in schools. It was comforting to realize that most of the teachers in whose classrooms I conducted research are affectionate and genuinely concerned with the complete well-being of their students.

In addition to the formality of adult-child interactions, the physical layout and classroom procedures convey to children their place in school culture. Norris Johnson (1985) discovered that teachers can convey much about the power structure of the classroom through nonverbal communication. I too have observed that in their interactions with teachers, children are forced to look up at the teacher from either a seated position on the floor or seated at a desk. This distance seems only to exaggerate the power adults have over children, and these clearly defined boundaries seem to strengthen the tacit organization of the school.

Teachers try to interact with children at a compromising eye level, and most teachers arrange their classrooms in ways that diminish the teacher's desk as the focal point of the room. In fact, most teachers use their desks more like a shelf, rather than as a point from which to teach. Children's tables are arranged in patterns that move away from the traditional rows of seats that one finds in the older grades.

For me, the toughest adjustment on entering school culture was relinquishing my freedom as an adult to make my own decisions. In the classroom, I had to abide by the class routines set in place by the teacher. In my fieldwork with children, I have primarily employed the method of participant observation. This method allows the researcher to view the culture from an insider's perspective, and I believe this is particularly important when trying to understand children's cultures (Dougherty, 1985; Fine, 1987; Kelly-Byrne, 1989; Tyler, 1969).

In class, I was treated as much as possible like a student and participated in all the children's daily activities (Holmes, 1995). There were times, however, when I did not want to do another worksheet or complete an assigned art project. Sometimes I wanted to color the circle red rather than the color recommended by the teacher. The children often shared these desires. I recall one art project where we were making owl puppets. The teacher (in whole group instruction) had requested that we make the body of the owl brown. James (seated on my right) leaned over and said, "I know it's supposed to be brown, but I like green. We can't use green, can we?" In these instances, it became clear that the task (the nature of the project) and the time frame (when it began and ended) were completely controlled by the teacher. Children have relatively little input in their own educational experiences, and are at the mercy of their teacher's scheduled routines and interactional styles (Wood, 1988). Some teachers are cognizant of this and give children power to make their own decisions regarding what colors to use, what activities to pursue next, or where to sit in the classroom.

Peer Culture

Although children are participants in a culture that is officially controlled by adults, there is an aspect of school culture that exists outside of the realm of adult control. This includes children's interactions with other children. Wherever children congregate, they share a culture that exists apart from the adult world (Corsaro & Eder, 1990; Konner, 1991). This is no less true for child-child interactions that occur on school premises. School is an institution that is maintained by adults, yet children manage to sustain and transmit cultural knowledge to their schoolmates, often unbeknownst to the very adults who are supposed to control them (Opie & Opie, 1984).

For example, in American schools, each grade has a designated curriculum it must follow. Such an arrangement does not appear to be cross-cultural. In many societies where traditional educational practices exist, children of several different age groups receive instruction as a group (e.g., Ahmed, 1983). The American educational system restricts peer interactions to those involving children of similar ages. Recess periods, if given, allow only several grades to play outdoors at the same time. In some schools, each grade had a clearly defined territory that is monitored by playground supervisors.

It is during these times of the day that children are free to associate with their peers with minimal adult intervention and supervision.[3] Thus, it is in these areas that peer culture thrives. During recess on the playground, children are free to interact with their peers. This is the children's domain, and it is one area where children's cultures and the transmission of cultural knowledge flourish. This is the time of the school day when children engage in mastering their culture and exerting their power in their world.

Consider, for example, verbal art forms such as the rhymes, stories, and jokes that permeate childhood. Some of the material

is passed down for several generations with little if any altera-
tion in content. An example of a historical verse that children
still chant in the schools is

> (Girl's name) and (boy's name) sittin' in a tree.
> K-I-S-S-I-N-G (letters pronounced individually).
> First comes love,
> then comes marriage,
> then comes the baby in the baby carriage.

Two years ago during the Christmas holidays, the kindergarten class I was visiting taught me the following altered lyrics
to the classic holiday song "Jingle Bells." This occurred during
our outdoor recess time.

> Jingle bells, Batman smells, Robin laid an egg.
> Batmobile lost its wheel, and Joker took ballet. Hey!

As a child, my own peer culture also invented lyrics to this
classic Christmas song and engaged in the cultural transmission of its material. I shared my verse with the children, and
these exchanges were some of the most enjoyable moments of
my fieldwork.

Other songs with altered lyrics address the children's school
experiences and the power differential between teachers and
students. For example, the following appears to be a popular
song the children sing on the bus to school. My niece and
nephews, who live about 10 miles from each other, also were
familiar with the following song:

> Row, row, row your boat, gently down the stream.
> Throw your teacher overboard and listen to her scream.

It seems reasonable to suggest that the process by which
children pass along cultural knowledge to their peers has re-

mained relatively stable over time. Through oral traditions passed on from older to younger members, children learn about their own social worlds and their place in the adult world.

To the best of my knowledge, most parents do not intentionally teach these versions of "Jingle Bells" or "Row, Row, Row Your Boat" to their children. Rather, children learn this knowledge from their peers and their siblings, and then share this information with other members (see also Guerra, 1989, and Konner, 1991). Through mechanisms such as the oral transmission of verbal art forms, children are able to sustain their own peer culture and maintain some control over their own behavior in an institution that, for the most part, is regulated by adults (see also Goodwin, 1997).

Bear in mind that the adult world and children's cultures are not so neatly separated. According to Opie and Opie (1984), children integrate material from the adult world into their culture. For example, the media is one of many socializing agents for children, and serves as a source from which children borrow material. Thus, what emerges from the rhymes and verses produced by children's cultures is their commentary about and attempts to make sense of the adult world.

Notes

1. American schools for the most part reflect European American, middle-class cultural ideals (Spindler & Spindler, 1990). This is beginning to change with the introduction and implementation of multicultural curriculums.

2. The emphasis on internalizing values of self-control and discipline stands in contrast to what is conveyed in some European schools (Spindler & Spindler, 1990).

3. The abolishment of children's rights, in particular their recess periods at school, has become a recent concern for child and play researchers (e.g., see Pellegrini, 1989, and Sutton-Smith, 1990). In all but two of the schools I visited, all the children enjoyed an outdoor recess period.

CHAPTER 4

Fieldwork and Gender

Before I began my fieldwork project investigating children's ethnic beliefs, I considered how my ethnicity might affect the research process. In agreement with Margery Wolf (1996), I believed that my skin color or ethnicity would neither preclude me from nor affect my ability to comprehend knowledge about children's social cognition gained through my experiences with them. I did not discount the fact that my ethnicity might in some way affect certain aspects of the process, however, such as my interactions with the children, school personnel, and adults in the communities where the schools were located. To this end, I mentioned peripherally the issue of matched ethnicity between me and the children in these projects.

Curiously, I never once considered the effect my gender would have on the fieldwork process. This occurred in spite of the fact that gender is a more salient classificational construct (than ethnicity) for young children, and one they employ regularly in attempting to order their social worlds. I maintained a gender-neutral position (Bell, 1993). I originally viewed a researcher's gender as a neutral factor that would not influence the fieldwork process when working with children. I presumed male and female researchers went about and experienced the fieldwork process in the same way, and that one's gender did not influence that process. As I read more of the literature on fieldwork and gender issues with adult communities, I began to notice the advantages and disadvantages of my own gender while conducting fieldwork with children on school premises. Consequently, my position on the relationship between gender and ethnography shifted.

According to Warren (1988), fieldwork and the resulting written text cannot be comprehended without considering how the researcher's gender affects this process (see also Bell et al., 1993; Geiger, 1990; Herod, 1993). Other researchers contend that a researcher's personal and life experiences affect fieldwork because the collection and interpretation of one's participants' experiences does not take place in a vacuum (e.g., Agar, 1986/ 1995; England, 1994; Hastrup, 1992). This parallels the work by Bem (1993), who views gender as a medium through which fieldwork experiences and interpretations of behavior are filtered. Cognitive science has brought forth the importance of contextualized bases of knowledge in explaining human behavior (Dougherty, 1985; Gardner, 1987, 1993). Similarly, ethnographic practice and theory would benefit from recognizing the role of contextualized knowledge and learning in the fieldwork experience (e.g., Bell, 1993). As Back (1993) suggests, gender is not simply a factor that affects methodological issues. Rather, it influences the way a fieldworker comes to know about the group he or she studies.

In agreement with Bem (1993), England (1994), and Hastrup (1992), I believe that my socialization experiences in childhood and life experiences in adulthood have guided either tacitly or overtly my field studies with children. In line with current thinking (Bronfenbrenner, 1986, 1989; Gardner, 1993; Turner & Bruner, 1986), I believe it is difficult to interpret behavior without acknowledging the contextual, ecological, and sociocultural factors in which it occurs in addition to those the fieldworker brings with him or her to the field. As a theoretical framework, I have adopted Bronfenbrenner's (1979a, 1979b, 1986, 1989) ecological approach to child development to explain the effect a fieldworker's characteristics have on the process when conducting research with children. In this chapter, I discuss how a fieldworker's gender affects methodological issues (e.g., establishing field relationships), data collection strategies, and interpretations of children's experiences. I proffer examples from my own fieldwork with children.

Sex Differences

One of the true documented anatomical differences between human males and females is that our species displays sexual dimorphism. Following puberty, males are typically larger and more muscular than females. In contrast, females are smaller and have a greater percentage of body fat than males (Jacklin, 1992; Maccoby & Jacklin, 1974). This anatomical difference has influenced the way children perceive and behave toward male and female fieldworkers.

For example, I am 5 feet, 4 inches tall. I find that my lack of physical presence gives me a distinct advantage in working with young children. I fit comfortably into the children's chairs and am able to play on their outdoor playground equipment without appearing clumsy. Children are no doubt intimidated by the adult world. Looking up at grown-ups is just another indication that children do not fit comfortably into the adult world and when they do, they are powerless (Corsaro, 1985; Fine & Sandstrom, 1988; Johnson, 1985; Oakley, 1994).

When working with children, female researchers may have an inherent size advantage over male researchers because they appear smaller and perhaps less intimidating and unthreatening (e.g., Codere, 1986; Golde, 1986; Morgen, 1989).[1] Overcoming adult authority is particularly important when working with children who perceive the adult-child relationship as one that inherently implies authority. I asked Brian, "What's the difference between kids and grown-ups?" He replied, "Grownups tell kids what to do, and kids have to listen." Male researchers, due to their traditionally larger physical presence, may have more difficulty circumventing this problem (or have to devise more ingenious ways) than typically smaller female researchers do. This potential disadvantage to male fieldworkers is compounded by the notion that females are viewed as being more accessible and less threatening, and having better communicative abilities as compared to men (e.g., Fischer, 1986; Golde, 1986; Mead, 1986; Warren, 1988; Whitehead & Conaway, 1986).

Young children are aware of and categorize their world on the basis of salient characteristics (e.g., Holmes, 1995; Mervis, 1987), and physical size is presumably an overt characteristic to which young children are sensitive. For example, although William Corsaro (1985) established a fine rapport with the nursery school children he studied, they nicknamed him "Big Bill." These children were obviously responding to the salient differences in physical size between adults and children. I suspect, however, that William Corsaro's size also could have been advantageous at times in his fieldwork with children, however.

Female researchers are also responsive and sensitive to the differences in physical size between children and adults. Barrie Thorne (1993) comments on how she felt like a big Alice trying to fit into scaled-down furniture during her research. It seems possible that when conducting fieldwork with children, a researcher's gender may influence this process directly because it is linked to how perceptions of adult authority may be interpreted by children through the fieldworker's physical presence.

A second genuine sex difference found in humans pertains to a form of play termed *rough and tumble*. By definition, rough-and-tumble play is characterized by play fighting that includes hitting, wrestling, and chasing with the intent of fighting (Goldstein, 1996; Hughes, 1995; Pellegrini, 1988). Contemporary ethological works define rough-and-tumble play as "a set of affiliative behaviors which include the exhibition of positive affect, vigorous movements, and reciprocal role playing" (Pellegrini, 1996, p. 108). One of the most consistently noted observations about the play of boys and girls is that rough-and-tumble play is the domain of boys (Pellegrini, 1985, 1988, 1996; Rubin, Fein, & Vandenberg, 1983). Cross-cultural evidence supports this sex differential (DePietro, 1981; Goldstein, 1996; Heaton, 1983; Whiting & Edwards, 1973).

Several lines of argument have been advanced to explain gender differences in rough-and-tumble play, namely, cultural influences and a biological predisposition. I shall pursue the former because it supports the theoretical framework advocated in this work. I do not dismiss the possibility that the interaction of cultural and biological factors may influence this behavior, however.

Studies with infants seem to support the contention that cultural factors (e.g., adult reinforcement for gender-appropriate behaviors) are responsible for the gender differential in rough-and-tumble play. Fagot, Hagan, Leinbach, and Kronsberg (1985) observe that adult reactions to infants' rough and aggressive behavior are dependent on the infant's sex. Female infants' aggressive behaviors are ignored, whereas male infants' aggressive behaviors provoke an adult reaction.

Further support for a cultural explanation emerges from studies on parent-infant play interactions (MacDonald, 1993).

Fathers are more likely than mothers to engage in rough-and-tumble play with their male and female infants (Parke & Tinsley, 1987). In addition, fathers are more likely to initiate rough play with their sons than with their daughters (Lamb, 1981). It is possible that children may receive both direct and indirect reinforcement for what is gender appropriate from adults in their environment. In this view, cultural-specific gender roles and societal attitudes about what is gender appropriate provide an explanation for the gender differential observed in rough-and-tumble play episodes. One final point deserves mention. Parent-infant interaction is a bidirectional process (Anderson, 1981; Maccoby, 1992; MacDonald, 1993). Thus, it seems reasonable to suppose that parents are responding to behavioral cues elicited by their male and female infants, and reciprocally provide different play patterns for them based on those cues.

As a form of children's play, rough-and-tumble play contains positive affective behaviors and reciprocal role taking that is found in many chase games and pretend play. Rough-and-tumble play also possesses an ingredient that other play does not, however—energetic physical activity (e.g., hitting, running, chasing; Pellegrini, 1996). Boys find this kind of activity particularly pleasing, whereas girls do not. Thus, because boys are drawn to this kind of activity, they consequently select other boys with whom to engage in rough-and-tumble play (Pellegrini, 1996). According to Maccoby (1986), this interest and preference in different kinds of activities leads to gender segregation.

If males are socialized to be more aggressive than females, and rough-and-tumble play is the dominion of boys, it is probable that most female researchers have had little opportunity or social experience in rough-and-tumble play. I rarely, if ever, engaged in rough-and-tumble play with any of the children in my studies. Female researchers may be at a disadvantage if this type of play is performed frequently by young male children. In this instance, the researcher would be excluded from participating in the play due to a variety of reasons, including: a) a lack of play competency, b) a dislike for this type of play activity and no desire to participate in it, c) rough-and-tumble play is not condoned by school personnel, and d) social values that constrain girls from engaging in rough-and-tumble play.

Participation by a female researcher in such activities would be presumably rare, and data, if collected at all, would be gathered primarily through other qualitative means. Such notions can be interpreted through the theoretical framework proposed by Bronfenbrenner (1979a, 1979b, 1986, 1989). The differential socialization and play experiences of male and female fieldworkers as children could potentially influence what phenomena in children's groups are observed and how data are collected as adult fieldworkers.

For example, it is possible that female fieldworkers who have had little exposure to rough-and-tumble play would opt to exclude this activity when observing children's play behavior. By contrast, because rough-and-tumble play is the domain of boys, male fieldworkers would have an advantage because they have had prior experience with and presumably were attracted to this kind of play as children. Thus, male researchers may be more inclined to focus on this particular aspect of children's cultures and play behaviors. The influence of gender in such hypothetical instances (i.e., male and female fieldworkers focusing on different cultural phenomena in the same children's culture) parallels the differential experiences of male and female fieldworkers working in adult communities (Fischer, 1986; Murphy & Murphy, 1985).

Also, age and gender are important factors in how one interprets acts of rough or aggressive play. According to Goldstein (1996), "aggressive play includes mock fighting, rough-and-tumble play, and/or fantasy aggression" (p. 127).

For example, children and adults possess different perceptions and consequently interpretations of aggressive play. Children are able to make a sharper distinction between rough play and real aggression. Adults have much more difficulty in distinguishing real aggression and children's aggressive play because adults impose their conceptions on the children's behavior (Fry, 1990; Pellegrini, 1988, 1996; Sutton-Smith, 1990; Wegener-Spohring, 1989). Children are aware that they are metacommunicating the message "this is play" and not engaging in real aggressive acts (Bateson, 1956).

Consistent findings also suggest that discrepancies exist between the way males and females interpret aggressive behavior and rough forms of play. Connor (1989) notes that females have more of a propensity to interpret rough or aggressive play as real aggression. In contrast, males are more likely to consider these rough acts as play. The interpretations of rough play episodes from women with prior experience in aggressive play as children parallel the interpretations of the men. Thus, it appears that the differential socialization and play experiences of males and females (and as they relate to gender) can affect how one interprets rough or aggressive play behavior. Male and female fieldworkers studying children's play who have not had prior experiences in particular play activities may be inclined to misinterpret children's aggressive play behaviors as real aggression.

For example, Barrie Thorne (1993) reveals that she felt closer to the girls during her research on school premises than she did the boys. Recollections of her own childhood allowed her to experience some familiarity with the gender-typed interactions and styles of play engaged in by the girls. Because she had little experience with the boys' activities as a child, she felt less familiar with them. Thorne also notes, however, that she was better able to analyze the play of boys because she was more detached from those activities.

Data Collection: Conducting Interviews

Participants' emic constructs of ethnicity and social class may attenuate a fieldworker's ability to establish a rapport with his or her community (e.g., Beoku-Betts, 1994). A fieldworker's gender can also create a barrier when attempting to establish rapport with respondents. There is a considerable literature base on the influence a researcher's gender has on the interview process (e.g., Axinn, 1991; Finch, 1984; Herod, 1993; Oakley, 1981; Williams & Heikes, 1993).

For example, Back (1993), a male fieldworker, discusses the difficulties he encountered in interviewing young adult female and male informants. Although interviewing groups of women posed no problem, conducting interviews with individual women was problematic. Young male community members interpreted the interview events as having sexual connotations. His interviews with male respondents were also influenced by gender. Issues of peer group status and hierarchy positions emerged during his interview sessions. In both instances, his gender affected the fieldwork and interview process.

In conducting interviews, women researchers are reported as being able to establish a greater rapport with their participants than male researchers because women are perceived as less threatening and having better communication skills. In addition, when conducting interviews, women are inclined to be more receptive to emotional communication than men (e.g., Codere, 1986; Fedigan & Fedigan, 1989; Golde, 1986; Warren, 1988; Whitehead & Conaway, 1986).

These advantages and skills come into play when conducting interviews in the field with children. In Chapter 2, "Methods: Working With Children," I suggest that structured individual interviewing is much too stressful for children and perceived by them as threatening or anxiety provoking

(Holmes, 1995). The interviews of choice for children are those employed in most fieldwork—unstructured and informal interviews (Bernard, 1994).

Open-ended interviews explore the children's views of their world and allow the researcher to devise hypotheses and generate theory (Reinharz, 1992). This method provides the investigator access to the children's thoughts, which are expressed in emic terms (Reinharz, 1992). Finally, open-ended interviews make the task of gathering information from children participants more intimate and familiar, both of which facilitate making them comfortable (Sexton, 1982).

For fieldworkers working with children in schools, unstructured and informal interviews can take place in a variety of places, including the hallways and cafeteria and during recess periods (Corsaro, 1985; Holmes, 1995; Reifel, 1986; Schofield, 1989; Thorne, 1993). In my own research, I have made extensive use of informal interviews during the children's playtime. During these periods, the children were engaged in pretend play scenarios or games of chase, and it was quite easy to enter into conversations with them and elicit answers to my queries. My ability to participate in pretend play activities was one distinct advantage that facilitated interviewing the children during playtime, however. One consequence of the socialization process females experience from infancy and through their childhood is that they become more adept than boys at social and communicative skills (e.g., Codere, 1986; Eisenberg, 1983; Fedigan & Fedigan, 1989; Golde, 1986; Warren, 1988).

For example, gender-appropriate toys and the toy preferences of children appear to indicate that girls are more inclined to play with toys that center on the home and domestic activities. These props facilitate the development of communication and social skills, and emphasize the importance of social relationships. By contrast, boys are more inclined to play with toys that center on construction, building, and sports. These props facilitate the development of mathematical and spatial skills

(Eisenberg, 1983; Schwartz & Markham, 1985; Tracy, 1987). My ability to establish a dialogue with the children and the ease with which I moved through the children's (boys and girls) various play activities enabled me to gather a wealth of interview material on children's cultures.

The researcher's gender may affect the interview process in other ways. For example, in the majority of schools I visited, administrative positions were occupied by males (e.g., Allan, 1993; Clifford, 1989; Goodman, 1992). The most important administrator in the primary and secondary school structure is the principal. For young children, the office of the principal often connotes authority and discipline. Perceptions of the principal are based on the context of the interaction, however. For example, bringing the attendance sheet to the principal's office in the morning is a treasured class chore. Being sent to the principal's office for misbehaving produces a different set of responses (Kohlberg, 1968, 1981).[2] Male researchers working with children may have to work harder at establishing rapport with them during the interview process because of the children's prior experiences with male authority figures, namely the principal. Thus, child researchers who make extensive use of interviewing should become sensitized to the children's negotiation of the gendered context of these interactions (Warren, 1988; Williams & Heikes, 1993).

Gender Identity

One of the most important tasks of childhood and adolescence is completing the process of identification successfully (Erikson, 1963, 1968). A particular aspect of the identification process is the acquisition of gender identity. Our gender identity influences how we think, feel, behave, are perceived by others, and perceive ourselves. Because this book addresses the influence of a researcher's gender and ethnicity on the field-work process (and offers socialization experiences as a partial explanation for this), I will provide a brief summary of theoretical perspectives on how one acquires gender identity.

Several theoretical perspectives explain the acquisition of gender identity. Two contemporary stances are social learning theory (Bandura, 1977; Kagan, 1971) and cognitive theories (Kohlberg, 1966; Bem, 1981, 1983, 1985). Social learning theory emphasizes the importance of observed behavior via imitation of a model in the acquisition of gender identity. By contrast, cognitive theories stress the importance of mental processes in acquiring gender identity.

Social learning theory contends that gender identification occurs through the process of observation and imitation of an adult model. According to this theory, children imitate the behaviors of a same-sex model and are reinforced for repeating these behaviors. This increases the probability that the child will perform these actions again. Social learning theory provides a partial explanation for how gender identification occurs. Criticisms of this view emphasize that children often imitate cross-sex models, do not imitate their parents at all, and may receive reinforcement for their own gender-typed preferences rather than their parents (Bandura, 1977; Kagan, 1971, 1984).

Two alternative cognitive theories explain the acquisition of gender identity—cognitive developmental theory (Kohlberg, 1966) and gender schema theory (Bem, 1981, 1983, 1985). In cognitive developmental theory, gender identity occurs through children's active classification of their own gender and organizing their behavior around that concept. According to Kohlberg (1966), this should occur in a particular sequence. For example, children have to be able to classify themselves as either boys or girls prior to organizing their behavior around that concept. Criticisms of this theory focus on the fact that children often act in gender-appropriate ways long before they have acquired the knowledge that their gender remains stable over time.

Finally, there is the gender schema theory proffered by Bem (1981, 1983, 1985) to explain the acquisition of gender identity. Seeing flaws in both the cognitive developmental and social learning approaches to gender identity acquisition, Bem combines elements of both to form a new theory of gender identity development. She contends that children socialize themselves in their own gender roles by organizing their behavior around a schema for gender. By observing what is appropriate for girls and boys in their own culture, the children subsequently adapt their own behaviors to fit those schema. This theory seems to receive support from children's actual behavior. During the socialization process, children presumably observe models in their culture, and then actively organize their own behavior to fit their schema for gender. Presumably, boys and girls operate according to different gender schema, which accounts for the differential socialization experiences that arise for men and women.

Gender Segregation

The sexual cleavage on the school playground that appears in the latter primary school years (e.g., Maccoby & Jacklin, 1987; Schofield, 1981; Thorne, 1993) is not as pronounced in young children. Maccoby (1990) explains sex segregation at play through preferential tastes, that is, one sex doesn't like the activities the other sex prefers to play, and the fact that boys don't respond to girls' wishes. Rather, boys seem to fulfill their own desires in play. As Thorne (1993) suggests, however, boys and girls do come together at times to play with one another in cross-sex groups. What is important is under what circumstances these cross-sex gatherings occur.

In nursery school and kindergarten, same- and cross-sex play groups are observed in almost equal proportions depending on contextual situations. Boys are inclined to join girls in playing house, and girls are likely to be found playing with boys in games of chase (e.g., Gesell & Ilg, 1946; Holmes, 1991; Maccoby & Jacklin, 1987; Sutton-Smith, 1979). Thus, in the early years, there are more opportunities for the sexes to play together because each sex is likely to prefer at least some of the games the other sex is playing.

Nevertheless, there are times when entrance to play groups is based exclusively on gender membership. Examples on school premises include class competitions divided along gender lines and play groups established by the children that allow access only to same-sex players (Holmes, 1991; Thorne, 1993). Thus, one's sex becomes an issue for children desiring access to certain play groups, and to researchers desiring to access particular aspects of a culture reserved typically for one sex (Bernard, 1994; Johnson, 1986; Warren, 1988; Werner & Schoepfle, 1987).

Access to Children's Cultures and a Fieldworker's Gender

Gaining access to children on school premises is not dependent on the fieldworker's gender, because these sites are not restricted in any way to either males or females. Field relationships with the adults in the school can be influenced by the researcher's gender, however. For example, Norris Johnson (1985), a male researcher who conducted fieldwork in an elementary school, experienced some initial friction from female teachers. He attributes this to what he calls "male hegemony"— when males employ female rather than professional status in an attempt to undermine female authority in social interactions.

Contemporary researchers argue that males have also experienced similar negative encounters in early childhood education (Cohen, 1990; Draper & Gordon, 1984; Robinson, 1988; Skeen, Robinson, & Coleman, 1986). As Cohen (1990) contends, few males voluntarily select careers that require them to engage in direct contact with young children. The overwhelming minority of men who enter into child care careers and primary school teaching appears to be a cross-cultural phenomenon (Kauppinen-Toropainen & Lammi, 1993). It seems plausible that these fields may be resistant to males, and hence males do not voluntarily select to enter into them.

Some males do voluntarily select nontraditional positions in child care and early childhood education, however (Williams, 1995). Positive images of males who work with young children are promoted in the early childhood literature (Cunningham, 1992a, 1992b). Also, the role of the male and how it is perceived by others in the field may dictate how he is treated. For example, a male early childhood teacher may experience prejudice in his field. A male researcher who is visiting the school may be perceived as either a desirable authority or a child advocate, however. Thus, gender is not the sole factor that guides the treatment of males in these fields. Rather, gender acts in concert with the role they fulfill.

In all the kindergarten classrooms I have visited, I have never encountered a male teacher. According to Williams (1995), teaching is a female-dominated vocation and linked to attributes associated typically with women, such as nurturance and emotional attachment. The trend in the schools I visited reflect general educational practice. Most of the teachers are female, and a large percentage of them are married (Rury, 1989; Williams, 1993). I never experienced the same kind of resistance from female teachers as Johnson (1985) did, and it brought to light that being a female researcher in a female-dominated profession probably had worked to my advantage.

Unlike access to field sites, access to children's cultures once inside the school is, at times, gender dependent (e.g., McKeganey & Bloor, 1991). I do not mean to imply that a fieldworker's gender is sufficient to ensure a fieldworker's access to all cultural activities in which participation is determined by gender (Davis, 1986; Friedl, 1986; Gonzalez, 1986). Rather, the researcher's gender may exclude or include his or her participation in a particular activity.

For example, Niara Sudarkasa (1986) was not privy to the social sphere of men in the Yoruba community she studied because she was a woman. Conversely, Johnson (1985) met with some initial resistance by female teachers because he shared gender membership with the principal. One should not infer that gender membership alone is sufficient to ensure access to all a gender's activities, however (Davis, 1986; Friedl, 1986; Gonzalez, 1986). Gender becomes an important and salient criterion that children use to allow or deny the fieldworker entrance into the play group.

For example, I can recall one play period when I was not permitted to join a same-sex girls' play group. During a free-play period, I asked a play group "boss" for permission to enter an indoor play group where five girls had just established an all-girls play group. I was denied access and not allowed to play with them. Wendy, Melissa, and Linda proclaimed, "We're all from the same neighborhood and you're not, so you can't play." Hence, my access to the group was denied by the children not on the criterion of gender but on residence location (see Corsaro, 1985, for a discussion of young children's access rituals into and strategies for denying entrance into play groups). In this instance, being female and the same gender as the play group members did not ensure my access to their play activities.

Some of the girls were organizing a play activity on the playground during recess before school began. Brian Patrick, a male classmate, approached and asked if he could play. Kendall replied, "No boys. This game is for girls." I was invited to play, and joined without any protest from the groups' members. Maria told me, "You could play too, Robyn 'cause you're a girl like us" (see Corsaro, 1985, for a discussion of players' access rituals and entrance refusals into play groups). Fine (1987), a male researcher, presumably experienced this same-sex advantage in his work with preadolescent males.

One might suspect that a researcher's attempt to gain access to children's play groups may be likened to anthropologists conducting interviews on topics that are taboo to discuss in adult mixed company. Thus, a fieldworker's gender affects his or her accessibility to certain groups and phenomena within a culture (e.g., Abu-Lughod, 1992; Murphy & Murphy, 1974; and Wolf, 1992, for females; and Agar, 1973 and Chagnon, 1977, for males). The parallels between adults' and children's societies with respect to access to certain activities based on gender membership ends here. My gender rarely prohibited me from entering any of the children's activities, and I was able to move freely through activities that were the dominion of boys and girls or that involved cross-sex participation.

For example, I was allowed to play in the boys' groups when no other girls were allowed because I wasn't a "real girl." When the boys were involved in a building activity or game of chase that was not open to the girls, I was still allowed to play. This occurred despite appeals from the girls that I was a girl, and they still let me play with them. The boys countered their pleas with the logic that I wasn't a real girl like their classmates, and thus I could play with them. This occurred in part because I was treated at times more like a treasured commodity or perhaps a "girlfriend," which gave the boys' group I was playing in some kind of elevated status. The children constructed and reconstructed my gender in the field, and it seems logical that when classifying me into the sociocultural category girl, the boys employed different criteria than they used for their chronological classmates (Bem, 1985; Briggs, 1986; Mervis, 1987).

My ability to move freely among both sexes during play was also due partly to the cognitive abilities of the children and my own play competencies. I was, in the children's estimation, a "good" player at different kinds of activities due to my own childhood participation in same-sex and cross-sex play activities. I was equally competent in play activities the boys enjoyed, such as chase, building with blocks, and basketball, and those enjoyed by the girls, such as house, jumping rope, and swinging. Thorne (1993) reveals that she felt closer to the girls of her study through memories of her own childhood. Her childhood experiences allowed her to access familiar gender-typed interactions and types of play for the girls, but not for the boys because she had little experience with their activities as a child. By contrast, I felt at ease and familiar with the gender-typed interactions and play of both sexes.

Alternatively, it seems reasonable to suppose that my ability to move freely through the play groups was influenced by the way the children categorized me based on my behavior and their own construction of gender schemata (e.g., Bem, 1985; Briggs, 1986). Here I am in agreement with Warren (1988), who views gender as one structural foundation on which the negotiation of one's research roles and identities rests. Through androgynous behavior and my interactions with the children, I learned ways to negotiate my way into as complete a participation in their culture as possible. Similarly, the children constructed and reconstructed my gender identity when I was with them.

Some male researchers may have more difficulty in participating in a wider range of children's play activities. This could be due to the fewer socialization experiences and opportunities they would have had as children to participate in primarily female play activities such as house and "baby" or jumping rope. It is well documented that boys are encouraged more than girls to engage in sex-typed play activities, and girls are given more latitude in selecting cross-sex toys (Eisenberg, Murray, & Hite, 1982; Eisenberg, Wolchik, Hernandez, & Pasternak, 1985; Langlois & Downs, 1980; Robinson & Morris, 1986; Tracy, 1987).

In addition, the literature suggests that women have better communication skills than men (Codere, 1986; Fedigan & Fedigan, 1989; Golde, 1986; Warren, 1988)—a necessary ingredient to be a successful player in pretend activities. Perhaps in these instances, androgynous ethnographers may have an advantage over stereotypical feminine and masculine ones.

Fieldwork and Gender

Evidence from the literature suggests that an investigator's gender affects the collection of data with adult populations (Bell et al., 1993; Bernard, 1994; Keller, 1985; Werner & Schoepfle, 1987; D. Wolf, 1996a), and this is no less true for conducting research with children. For example, one of the many factors discussed in this work is the influence of the fieldworker's gender on accessibility to certain children's groups and activities. More important to the advancement of ethnography is how a researcher's personal traits affect the fieldwork process with children.

Consider Karl Heider's (1988) work that addresses the underlying causes as to why ethnographers disagree about their interpretations of similar cultures (see also Agar, 1986/1995). The issue, perhaps with respect to gender, is not one of methodological differences or contrasting views, as was the case for Fischer (1986) and Goodenough (1956, 1957) on Truk society. Rather, it is one of dual perspectives that emerges in the work of Robert and Yolanda Murphy (1985) and Daisey Dwyer (1978) and her spouse Kevin Dwyer (1982), and how ethnographers come to know about the cultures they study. Several researchers (Bleier, 1984; Fee, 1986; Gilligan, 1982; Keller, 1985) suggest that women scientists view the world differently from men, and thus practice their science and approach their subject matter in a distinctive matter.

Before continuing, I am compelled to state that I do not believe that any of the following contentions are due to any innate differences between men and women. Several works contend that women are better at fieldwork and suited more to qualitative methods because of their ability to empathize, share, and enter into nonhierarchical relationships in the field (Fedigan & Fedigan, 1989). I believe neither that women are better at fieldwork simply because they are women nor that only women and not men possess such qualities or attributes (see also D. Wolf, 1996a, 1996b). Rather, I see the differences in perspectives as arising from the often disparate socialization experiences of human beings based on membership in a particular gender group (Bem 1993; Keller, 1985; Rowell, 1984; D. Wolf, 1996a, 1996b).

The different socialization experiences of males and females may be viewed within the theoretical framework of the cultural ecological model proposed by Bronfenbrenner (1986, 1989). Within this framework, an individual's behavior and how he or she comes to know about the world are influenced by ecological and cultural factors that shape an individual's life experiences. For example, contemporary women, like their colonial ancestors, are socialized to be moral, nurturant, devoted, and affectionate (Chafe, 1992). By contrast, contemporary males are socialized to be aggressive, dominant, and adventurous (Williams & Best, 1990). Such factors are partly responsible for the differing perceptions that men and women have about the world.

As Nast (1994) suggests, women are associated with child-rearing tasks that concern, among other issues, the child's physical well-being. This appears to be a cross-cultural universal. As Oakley (1994) notes, women are linked to children through childbirth, and this connection extends into social and cultural domains. Children belong to women and become socially aligned with them. It is not surprising then that an overwhelming number of female scholars have engaged in topics such as early childhood education, children's play, children's rights, and the study of childhood—subject areas that allow the connection between women and children to be strengthened. It appears to be a bidirectional connection. Women are linked to children, and children as participants attract women researchers.

This link between children and women surfaces in how a fieldworker's gender can affect establishing a rapport with young children. For example, the category of mother is associated with nurturing qualities, and these can come into play during fieldwork (Rosch, 1973; Warren, 1988). This was confirmed in my research.

It would be unjust to presume that only female researchers can be empathetic and nurturing, whereas male researchers cannot possess these qualities. Rather, my position is that women in general and American women in particular have been socialized to possess these traits, whereas men as a social group have not (see Bem, 1993; D. Wolf, 1996b).

Nursery school and kindergarten teachers, who are predominantly females, perform many roles. One of these is substitute mother (Granucci, 1990). In the early years, children's experiences with female teachers provide them with an initial affective relationship that resembles the mother-child bond. Because women in our society are customarily associated with nurturance, the preschool teacher is categorized as mother because she exhibits similar behaviors (Johnson, 1985).

As Warren (1988) suggests, the children draw on their experiences and classify the fieldworker based on his or her personal qualities, behavior, and interactions with them. In structuring the category females, young children come to view all females as possessing the attributes of their prototypical female— mother—who is presumably caring and nurturing (Kagan, 1984; Mervis, 1987; Rosch, 1973). Social psychological literature suggests that children structure their categories and the members included in them around the principle of homogeneity

(Holmes, 1995; Mervis, 1987; Tajfel, 1982). Thus, because I am an older female, I must be a mother (e.g., Kagan, 1984).

Accordingly, I have noticed in my fieldwork that some children tend to address female adults by the prefix "Mrs.," presumably because they also believe all female adults are married. When working with children, female fieldworkers are able to adopt and negotiate various research identities and roles that include friend, substitute mother, classmate, and grown-up depending on the context of the interaction. This flexibility of roles and identities is an advantage when working with children because it extends the boundaries and contexts in which one can interact and establish a trusting relationship.

According to Nast (1994), women typically are associated with nurturance and caregiving, and are hence linked to the physical care of children. Thus, it was no surprise the children sometimes approached me seeking nurturance or caretaking assistance. I was frequently asked to button coats, help zip knapsacks and tie shoes, and put barrettes in the children's hair—requests that were never directed at peers. One of my most embarrassing moments while conducting research occurred when a male classmate, Richard, exited the bathroom and asked me to help him buckle his belt. Aware of school policy about touching the children, I pondered momentarily as to whether I should help Richard with his request because the teacher was not nearby. Nevertheless as his "best friend," I did not want to compromise our relationship. Implicit in this rule-governed relationship (e.g., Argyle & Henderson, 1985) is that you help a friend in need. Apparently, my response to his request was far too slow for him, because Richard said loudly, "Robyn could you hurry and help me with my pants? The girls are coming." I knelt down quickly and helped him buckle his belt. Such experiences and interactions with the children strengthened our relationship because they facilitated the development of mutual trust and security in a variety of contexts.

Although individual males may possess a gentle and nurturing style in interacting with young children, males as a group, and by extension male fieldworkers, are rarely recognized for their nurturing qualities (Lamb, 1987; Rane & Draper, 1995). This general trend has extended into the American educational system, and is reflected in the vocational choices of men and women. Although males may occupy administrative positions in education and teach in the latter primary and secondary grade levels, few males have been attracted to early childhood education (Allan, 1993; Cohen, 1990; Kauppinen-Toropainen & Lammi, 1993). My experiences and observations in contemporary primary schools confirm a similar trend. There is a relatively recent influx of males, however, who are selecting teaching as their vocation and who are voluntarily choosing to teach the primary grades.[3]

It seems reasonable to suppose that American cultural ideals and values and differential socialization processes are discouraging males from nurturing children. Yet it is precisely these nurturing behaviors that young children seek out in their preschool and kindergarten teachers, and these behaviors and skills should be beneficial to men when working with young children. Male teachers should not have to endure the threats of child molestation associated with males who select careers that involve contact with children.[4]

The above discussion on how a fieldworker's gender may influence the relationship he or she establishes with child participants is based on the notion that children seek out nurturing qualities in females and appear to respond favorably to them. Thus, gender affects how fieldworkers establish a rapport with their child participants. It is equally likely that a child may not seek out these same qualities in the friend role relationships of participant observation, however. Rather, gender may work in concert with other characteristics such as playfulness, access to resources, and lack of rejection not related to a fieldworker's gender but to interactional styles.

Fedigan and Fedigan (1989) posit that female researchers have a predilection to respect individual differences and develop an intense emotional investment with their subjects (Fossey, 1983; Goodall, 1986). This is particularly true of the way I view and approach the children's groups I study. I perceive them as individual members with distinct personalities who constitute a larger group that collectively shares cultural knowledge. More important, I do not dismiss individuality as simply interindividual variation. I explore each child's uniqueness to expand the description and interpretation of the culture. I employ informal or unstructured interviewing because this method produces unconventional information that permits me to make use of interindividual differences (Reinharz, 1992).

It is possible that male researchers studying children's groups focus on the whole rather than on individual children, perhaps as a consequence of the different peer socialization process experienced by boys and girls. It is a well-documented fact that boys tend to engage in group play activities that involve numerous players, whereas girls are more inclined to partake in more dyadic play activities and relationships (Collins, 1984; Maccoby, 1990; Thorne, 1993). Such early experiences may contribute to different perceptions and interpretations of children's cultures by male and female researchers.

Additionally, evidence suggests that male and female fieldworkers studying adult communities focus on different phenomena in the same culture (e.g., Dwyer, 1978; Dwyer, 1982; Murphy & Murphy, 1985). It may be equally true that male and female fieldworkers might be focusing on different aspects of children's culture. Due to their own socialization experiences as children, adult researchers may be uncomfortable studying and engaging in certain kinds of play activities. It is well-documented that boys are socialized more intensely with regard to sex-typed activities than girls (Jacklin, 1992; Maccoby & Jacklin, 1974). In fact, by age 2, boys and girls play differently and prefer gender-appropriate playthings and activities (Caldera,

Huston, & O'Brien, 1989). This may affect the kinds of activities a researcher selects and limit the kinds of observations made.

For example, girls are more flexible than boys with respect to the toy preferences and sex-typing of toys. Girls are much more likely to play with "boys' toys" than boys are to play with "girls' toys" (Almquist, 1989). This is a consequence of the fact that boys are socialized more intensely than girls with respect to sex-typed behaviors. Hence, women researchers as a group are perhaps more likely and willing to engage in same-sex as well as cross-sex activities. They may be able to experience and interpret correctly a wider range of children's behaviors. Male or female researchers who are strongly sex-typed would most likely have difficulty engaging in the activities of the other gender due to inadequate childhood socialization experiences and opportunities for play with the opposite sex. In addition, it seems reasonable to suppose that limited exposure to particular play opportunities during childhood could affect the adult fieldworker's experiences and perceptions when studying children's behaviors.

Consider rough-and-tumble play as a topic of scholarly inquiry. Most female researchers have had little experience in this kind of play because it appears to be the province of boys (Fagot et al., 1985; Goldstein, 1996; Pellegrini, 1996). In fact, girls are typically socialized not to engage in this kind of play. It is not surprising that few female researchers have shown an interest in studying rough-and-tumble and other types of aggressive play. Most of the existing literature on these topics is produced by male researchers (Connor, 1989; Pellegrini, 1988, 1989; Sutton-Smith, 1988). Here a fieldworker's gender can directly affect the topic of inquiry selected for investigation and how data are interpreted (Connor, 1989). Androgynous fieldworkers may have an advantage over stereotypical masculine and feminine ones in this case. The former researchers would presumably be able to participate in a variety of play activities rather than those esoteric to same-sex play groups.

Keller (1987) suggests that women researchers are inclined to be more holistic and integrative as a result of differential socialization experiences. Hence, they are presumably more attuned to the subtleties of human social interaction. Research from children's toy preferences suggests that props for girls place more emphasis on social relationships than props for boys do (Eisenberg, 1983). This emerges in my own analysis of childhood cultures. I have abandoned the reductionist approach to concentrate on the subtleties of behavior of individuals and specific relationships. I search for patterns in the children's thinking rather than relying on descriptions of their behavior. I am more interested in a detailed understanding of children's cultures than in making sweeping generalizations (Fee, 1986; Turner & Bruner, 1986). In such instances, the interpretation and analysis of data may be affected by the interaction of the fieldworker's gender and his or her theoretical objectives (e.g., emic versus etic goals).

In ethnographic interpretation, I am more inclined to let the facts speak for themselves. When working with children, one needs to listen patiently to what the children have to say rather than operating with an a priori agenda (Fedigan & Fedigan, 1989). This is a common theme in feminist research, and it emerges in how I interview the children. I ask open-ended questions and conduct informal interviews while the children are drawing for me. I let the children lead and the material guide me (Fedigan & Fedigan, 1989). Patience and perseverance are required to interview young children. Children are great storytellers, and one needs to wait until the precise moment when the information can be gathered. When interviewing young children, the researcher needs to be patient and willing to wait for the desired information because the children are in control. Persistence, perseverance, and a willingness to engage in non-hierarchical field relationships appear to be desirable traits women and men fieldworkers possess (Fedigan & Fedigan, 1989; D. Wolf, 1996a).

Also, there is the notion that women researchers are able to empathize with the subjects they study. It is believed that women researchers resonate their feelings onto their subjects to understand them better (Fee, 1986; Fossey, 1983; Goodall, 1986). In my analysis of children's cultures, one of my primary goals is to move away from the simple recording of children's behavior. Rather, I attempt to interpret the children's behavior and conversations through subjective feelings and meanings (e.g., Turner & Bruner, 1986). The richness of children's cultures is derived from material about specific relationships, experiences, and the connections children make to other people in the children's social world. This emerges in the works of other female fieldworkers such as Stack (1974), Goodwin (1990), and Kelly-Byrne (1989). This material allows the fieldworker access into the subjective feelings and experiences of children, and ultimately the children's culture.

For women fieldworkers, subjectivity is a double-edged sword. Female fieldworkers often interpret data using the subjective feelings and experiences of the individuals and groups they study. In addition, women fieldworkers as a group are more willing than male fieldworkers to acknowledge their own subjectivity in the fieldwork process.

Similar issues have arisen in fieldwork with adult participants. Although Carol Stack (1974) and Elliot Liebow (1967) studied the African American community, they elected to study different aspects of the same phenomena and employ different perspectives. Stack concentrates on the connections and social networks that exist between the women in the community using their subjective feelings and experiences. By contrast, Liebow concentrates on individual men on the street corner and gives little attention to other individuals in the men's social lives. It seems reasonable to suppose that the different perspectives and selected focal aspects of each study are related in part to the fieldworker's gender and the differential socialization experiences of men and women.

Finally, and with regard to empathy for the children, I acknowledge that I have given, on occasion, more attention to children who were rejected by their peers or experiencing a crisis in their lives. Such "confessional" tales often appear in ethnographic works, particularly those written by female field-workers (Bell, 1993). One cannot help feeling sympathetic toward children who have been abused or are unable to make friends. It is impossible, I think, to remain detached when working with children in the field, although this is rarely acknowledged in the written text. These responses in no way had a negative effect on my fieldwork. Rather, they helped establish a rapport with children whose experiences might not otherwise be included. These children could be likened to exceptional cases, and are not dismissed by women researchers (Fee, 1986).

With respect to emotional investment, I care deeply for the children I study. Most, if not all, researchers become emotionally attached to the group of people they study. Some fieldworkers become possessive and when describing their group to others use phrases such as "my village" or "my kids." In my own experiences and as mentioned in Chapter 3, "School Organization and Culture," I became involved in the lives of the disadvantaged children with whom I conducted fieldwork. So too were some of their teachers. Protecting participants from harm and ensuring their well-being was extended to include the children's life experiences outside the school.

Children are powerless and defenseless in most interactions in the adult world. Fieldworkers who conduct research with children (whether privileged or disadvantaged) may find it difficult to take a detached stance during (and sometimes after) the fieldwork period. Yet this admission rarely finds it way into the final ethnographic text. I also passed over the subjective aspects of my field experiences in my earlier works.

For example, I stated previously that I was compelled to nurture and care for the children with whom I conduct fieldwork. The privileged children received primarily my attention on school premises. My attention to disadvantaged children crossed the boundaries of school and home, however. I brought them food, clothes, toys, and other necessities whenever I could. I made requests in my university classes for clothes donations for impoverished children. I knew these acts of reciprocity in which I was compelled to engage would not change the children's lives, however.

In this respect, there are several levels on which fieldworkers can assist the children they study. First, there is the personal level that includes how the fieldworker might offer reciprocity to the children he or she studies. Such acts may include bringing food, clothing, and other necessities to them. The next level includes enlisting the help of the community and other various institutions such as the school board, the YMCA, and the division of youth and family services. Last there is policy writing—a political level of involvement that is concerned with the children's welfare (Boyden, 1990).

Researchers working with homeless populations, third-world populations, and disadvantaged subjects probably experience the same desire to make the lives of the people they study better (e.g., D. Wolf, 1996a, 1996b). I do not view these actions as prejudicial to the fieldwork in any way. Instead, I think they add an important dimension to the cultures. Such actions have led me to take into account the children's whole life experiences and my own emotions while working with them. Some may argue that such disclosures are simply cathartic confessions. I contend that this type of behavior is more profound than simply a confession, and is guided by a variety of factors such as age of the participants studied and the fieldworker's gender and life experiences.

In conclusion, a fieldworker's gender affects the fieldwork process with children. His or her gender affects: a) the relationships established with the children (i.e., the children's perceptions of authority are linked to physical presence—males are larger and hence perceived as more threatening than females, who are typically smaller in stature), b) the collection and interpretation of certain cultural phenomena (e.g., rough-and-tumble play), c) interviewing strategies and techniques, d) access to certain cultural phenomena whose entrance is determined exclusively by gender membership, e) the ability to participate in certain kinds of children's activities as a consequence of socialization experiences, f) the desire to nurture child participants, and g) the perceptions of children's cultures as a consequence of differential socialization experiences for men and women.

Notes

1. There are of course certain fieldwork situations in which tall stature or lack thereof can be either advantageous or disadvantageous. For example, Turnbull (1968) comments on how his height affected his ability to move through the forest.

2. Views of the principal as a disciplinarian appear to be a function of age and cognitive maturity, although there is most likely an interplay of other various factors. Elementary school principals have devised creative ways to alter children's perceptions of the principal as disciplinarian.

3. At my university, I have noticed a relatively recent increase in male education majors. I am not certain whether this is specific to our institution or part of a national trend.

4. It is true for the general population that an overwhelming percentage of child molestation instances involve males, but this pattern does not hold true in child care environments.

CHAPTER 5

Fieldwork and Ethnicity

Researchers acknowledge the importance of personal traits such as gender, ethnicity, age, and social status in facilitating and guiding the fieldwork process (Agar, 1986/1995; Bell et al., 1993; Heider, 1988; Plumbo, 1995; Van Maanen, 1988; Warren, 1988). How adults in general, and fieldworkers in particular, conceive of and interact with children is dependent on culturally specific child-rearing practices, values, and expectations of child behavior. These emic concepts and behaviors guide the fieldworker's actions, and are neither useful nor appropriate when applied in other cultural contexts (Stevenson, Azuma, & Hakuta, 1986). This chapter addresses the influence that a researcher's ethnicity has on the collection and interpretation of data from children's cultures.[1]

Piaget (1929) established that children's thinking is qualitatively different from that of adults. Children, particularly young children, do not order their social universe using the same criteria adults do. Hence, the cultural specific and comparative terms for ethnic groups used by social scientists and adults do not hold much meaning for children (Holmes, 1995). By contrast, gender is a powerful sociocultural construct that young children recognize and employ in organizing their behavior and social universe (Bem, 1983). Thus, it seems plausible that children may attend more to a fieldworker's gender than to his or her ethnicity. In contrast, for the adult fieldworker, gender and ethnicity may be equally significant in the process.

Recent works in cross-cultural and multicultural research have addressed the need for scientists to recognize the influence that their ethnic or cultural identity has on their research activities. Multicultural counseling in particular has brought this issue to light (e.g., Helms, 1993; Pedersen, 1993; Sue, 1993). Fieldworkers working with young children also need to consider how their own ethnicity affects the fieldwork process.

As Agar (1980, 1986/1995) contends, one of the most difficult tasks faced by fieldworkers is to overcome their own cultural background so that they may be objective in their interpretive task. Attempts to discard one's cultural heritage in the field and the subsequent writing about one's field experience are compounded by methodological problems brought to the forefront by cross-cultural researchers. These include the difficulty and danger in transporting concepts and methods to study cultural happenings from one culture to another (e.g., Lasater & Johnson, 1994), and the notion that individuals from different cultures may focus on different facets of the same event (Azuma, 1986).

The concepts and theories employed in the social sciences were generated by western researchers (Azuma, 1986). Thus, they are most suitable when applied to cultures with similar ideologies. These paradigms are not an efficient or accurate means to study behavior and cognition in cultures in which these frameworks were not created. The need to devise accurate and useful standards of cross-cultural measurement has generated recent publications on this topic (Ember, 1994, in press).

In this chapter, I focus on mainstream European American, African American, East Indian, and Japanese culture to illustrate the possible effects that a researcher's ethnicity (cultural heritage) and the misuse of comparative constructs in cross-cultural research can have on the fieldwork process with children. This material is integrated into each of the groups discussed. Each group is preceded by views on children and childhood because these ideas are potential factors that can affect the fieldworker's interactions with and interpretations of children's cultures.

This material should be digested with the following points in mind. First, in this work, *culture* is viewed as knowledge shared collectively by members of a group. These internal representations contain rules and schemas for culturally appropriate behavior in domains such as family structure, child rearing, gender, and kinship (see Dougherty, 1985; Goodenough 1956, 1957; Harkness, 1996). This knowledge is linked to a society's worldview and plays a role in the group's survival. Although this knowledge is possessed by the group, differences in cultural competency between and within individuals are acknowledged. The term *ethnic group* is used to refer to individuals who acknowledge a common identity and participate in a shared cultural value system (Barth, 1992). Characteristics of the ethnic group are not possessed uniformly by all group members. Intragroup and intraindividual variation are respected (Orbe, 1995).

Second, the United States is a multicultural society. This cultural diversity is reflected in the numerous subgroups that shape American culture. The discussion on American culture recognizes this diversity, and mainstream, European American core values are presented as expansive terms shared by other ethnic groups. Julian and McKenry (1994) note that the three predominant minority ethnic groups in the United States (African American, Asian American, and Latino subgroups) share the same aspirations, values, and goals as middle-class, European Americans, while also disseminating cultural values and knowledge specific to the ethnic group.

Third, a fieldworker's ethnicity should not preclude him or her from acquiring and interpreting knowledge gained through children's experiences (e.g., Allen, 1991; Back, 1993; Stack, 1974; M. Wolf, 1996). Rather, one's cultural heritage tacitly or overtly guides the process and the substance of the field experience.

The material that follows is situated in the cultural ecological framework model by Bronfenbrenner (1979a, 1979b, 1986, 1989). He suggests that to understand a child's development, one needs to consider the importance and influence of ecological contexts on the child's development. Similarly, his notion of the importance of multilevel ecological contexts in a child's development is extended to the process of fieldwork. The levels that are most relevant to the fieldwork process are the macrosystem and the microsystem. The macrosystem is a broad ecological context that includes the ideologies and attitudes of a culture such as religious beliefs, notions about child rearing and ethics. The microsystem contains situations and environments that immediately and directly affect an individual such as the home, school, work setting, and neighborhood. These two systems will prove to be fruitful in examining the effect of a fieldworker's cultural or ethnic membership on the fieldwork process.

American Society

American Conceptions of Childhood

Like the concept of culture, childhood is a sociopsychological construct whose application and meaning are culture specific (Postman, 1982). By extension, conceptions of children, the place of children in a society, and expectations for their behavior are also culture-specific constructs (Yamamura, 1986). Societal views of childhood and children are mutable, and these concepts are susceptible to historical, cultural, social, and biological forces (Garbarino, 1986; Hawes & Hiner, 1985). More important, conceptions of children and childhood often vary within the same historical period, cultural group, and individual (Hwang, Lamb, & Sigel, 1996). These images and conceptions of children are linked to how fieldworkers view children's cultures.

Fieldworkers from the United States are influenced in part by the historical, social, cultural, and economic forces embedded in past and contemporary American culture.[2] Thus, American images of children and childhood are influenced to a degree by their western historical counterparts. Western notions toward children and about childhood have shifted considerably over the last few centuries, and changing ideas about children appear to coincide with specific historical periods (Brown, 1995).

In medieval Europe, historians have claimed that children were viewed as miniature adults, and no distinction was made between adults and children (Aries, 1962). This view has been successfully refuted. In the Enlightenment, Locke's *tabula rasa* led to the notion of experiential learning. This was used to validate the view that adults need to care for and nurture children (Postman, 1982). Religious beliefs of the time called for the firm discipline of discipline and a strong work ethic (Hughes, 1995).

Rousseau captured the views of Romanticism and viewed children as innately good and innocent (Postman, 1982). He believed children are not miniature versions of adults, but rather that children should be appreciated for who they are. The philosophies of Locke and Rousseau serve as the foundation for contemporary American views on developmental study (Hughes, 1995).

In 17th-century America, children were vital economic resources (Beales, 1985; Hareven, 1992), and were viewed as
adults in progress (Schneider, 1995). Childhood was seen as
preparation for adulthood, and this was reflected in play theories such as Groos's (1901) "play as practice for adulthood." The
view of childhood as a carefree time prevails in mainstream
American culture (Hunt & Frankenberg, 1990).

By the 19th century, children were seen as requiring adult
protection and supervision, and children were segregated from
the adult world. Changing attitudes of childhood were linked
to economic factors. Children were no longer viewed as an
essential part of the labor force. They were now viewed as
objects of nurturance that needed adult protection (Hareven,
1992). Children were believed to represent the future, a view
that has been rekindled in recent years (Finkelstein, 1985). The
Lockean view that children need care and protection is still
reflected in contemporary American culture (Postman, 1982).

Contemporary Views of Childhood

In the 20th century, children have been viewed as creatures
who need to be loved. This is due in part to the emergence of
developmental psychology, which emphasizes the emotional
and psychological well-being of the child (Ashby, 1985). According to Elkind (1987), American children are viewed as a
blessing, to be loved and admired for their childlike qualities,
yet they are also viewed as lacking discipline (remnants from
our Puritan past). Americans are often accused of trying to
prolong the period of childhood.

Some contemporary Americans make the distinction between the sentimental qualities of childhood and the realities of
how children experience childhood. For Coleman (1961), the
division between childhood and the adult world is so pronounced
that he titled his work *The Adolescent Society* to emphasize that
children are members of their own society that exists apart from

the adult world. As Hunt and Prout (1990b) suggest, the separation of childhood from the adult world is still the prevailing depiction of children. Such a notion presupposes that childhood exists in a vacuum, and during this period, children have no contact with adults. These authors contend that no attention is given to the historical, cultural, and social contexts in which childhood narratives exist.

Whatever one's beliefs, American children experience many different kinds of childhood (Lynott & Logue, 1993). In fact, experiences of childhood, like those of the researchers who describe it, are dependent deeply on gender, class, ethnicity, and geography (Berrol, 1985; Hunt & Prout, 1990b; Schneider, 1995). This holds true cross-culturally. Children all over the world have different experiences of childhood as a consequence of gender, class, ethnicity, and religious beliefs.

The past decade has brought about a shift in views on children and childhood. Many activities that distinguished children and adults in previous decades now have fuzzy boundaries (Kempton, 1981; Rosch, 1973). For example, children and adults now share similar clothing, games, and activities. One needs only to enter a large department store to see that children's clothes and shoes resemble adult wear in miniature— Weebooks are child-sized versions of Reebok sneakers, and Guess manufactures children's clothing to resemble its adult line. Calvin Klein has made extensive use of teen models who exude childhood innocence yet strike sensual poses.

The play of children has also been affected by changing cultural conceptions of childhood. In the 1940s and 1950s, children's play territories were their neighborhoods, and formalized play was limited. Play was child initiated and in the child's control (Postman, 1982). Contemporary children no longer play in neighborhoods. Cultural, social, historical, and economic factors have affected children's play territories, and play has moved to formal playing fields and indoors into demarcated play zones (e.g., Playdiums, Gymborees).[3]

Further, some forms of play that were once child initiated are no longer in children's control. Contemporary children now play in formal sports leagues (e.g., Little League and Tee-Ball) organized by adults. More important, play has moved from being motivated intrinsically to being motivated extrinsically according to adult and societal standards. Some children no longer play because it is fun. Rather, they play for extrinsic rewards (Postman, 1982). This appears to be supported by the increasing number of adolescents who enter professional sports. Contemporary parents spend more time transporting their children to events than they do interacting with them.

This change in the cultural conception of childhood has been influenced by a variety of factors. First, there is a genuine distinction between idealized, romantic views of childhood and the realities of childhood in contemporary American society (e.g., Hunt & Prout, 1990a, 1990b). Second, as Elkind (1995) contends, changes in cultural conceptions of children and child-hood are linked to changes in family structure. The following is a synopsis of Elkind's work.

From the mid-19th to the mid-20th century, the typical American modern family consisted of a nuclear family in which parents and their children resided in one household. The father was the sole economic provider, while the mother remained at home. Family members were dependent on one another, and time was set aside for the whole family to interact as a group. Love led to a monogamous marriage, and family obligations superseded individual pursuits. Children were seen as inno-cent and in need of adult protection. This was a return to the romantic view of childhood.

From 1960 to the present, the postmodern family arrange-ment has prevailed. This includes two-parent, single-parent, and adoptive families. Shared parental responsibilities and in-dependent family relationships are the norms. Individual goals are not sacrificed for family needs (see also Hareven, 1992). For most families, there is no longer a family supper hour. Family members remain part of a group, but independence is a guiding principle. Childhood competence and resiliency have replaced the romantic, carefree days of modern family notions of childhood (Elkind, 1995).

In our society, childhood is supposed to be a protected time for children. Children are expected to be shielded from the demands of economic, political, and sexual influences (Garbarino, 1978). The notion of the "hurried child," however, implies that U.S. children are viewed as too adult-like (Elkind, 1981; Packard, 1983; Winn, 1983). Children are experiencing parental pressure to achieve recognition and become interested in adult activities and endeavors (Hunt & Frankenberg, 1990). More important, the world's children do not experience the traditional, Western conception of childhood as carefree and innocent (Hunt & Prout, 1990a). Across the globe, there are homeless children, children living in areas affected by war, and children sold as slaves and prostitutes.

In an age of increased divorce, children are expected and called on to provide their parents with emotional support (Winn, 1983), a consequence of the postmodern family, where the view of childhood competence prevails (Elkind, 1995). Children are also experiencing more adult problems than ever before: Teen pregnancy, substance abuse, alcoholism, and criminal behaviors are just some examples. The pursuit of the American ideal of achievement is being pushed on children at earlier ages.[4]

American fieldworkers, like conceptions of childhood, are also susceptible to cultural, historical, and social forces. Additionally, fieldworkers are influenced by their own life experiences. Herein lies the advantage of interpreting the influence of a fieldworker's personal traits on the fieldwork process using the macrosystem and microsystem as proposed by Bronfenbrenner (1986, 1989). This theory takes into account how development is shaped by personal and general experiences from various environments in which the individual interacts. Fieldworkers in general, and American fieldworkers in particular, cannot escape the influence of their macrosystem on what they observe and how they interpret data from children's cultures.

Consider how a fieldworker's microsystem might affect the fieldwork process. For example, American fieldworkers (depending on their age) may have been raised in modern, postmodern, or some combination of these two family structures. Because each family structure is associated with a different view of children, fieldworkers raised in such households have had different socialization experiences and enter into the fieldwork process with different preexpectations and conceptions of children, childhood, and children's relationships. As Oakley (1994) suggests, childhood memories invade adult perceptions of childhood. Thus, memories and experiences enter into one's interpretations of childhood and children's behaviors.

American Culture, Individualism, and Fieldwork

Cross-cultural researchers have devised several dimensions with which to study cultural variation. One of these dimensions is individualism-collectivism (Dion & Dion, 1993; Triandis, 1989; Triandis & Berry, 1981; Triandis et al., 1988). Individualism is characteristic of cultures that place personal or individual goals and needs above those of the group. By contrast, collectivism is characteristic of cultures that place the goals and needs of the group (e.g., extended family) above individual needs and benefits (Triandis et al., 1988).

According to this definition, American culture is decidedly an individualistic one (Engel, 1988; Triandis & Berry, 1981; Wheeler, Reis, & Bond, 1989), and American fieldworkers working with children are also presumably guided by individualistic ideals. This is true of the complete fieldwork experience. It reflects the western ideology of individualism. Fieldwork is to some extent a lonely practice. It is a solitary endeavor in which an individual seeks to understand another group, and then convey that understanding to an audience of readers. Researchers entering the field are guided by personal goals and motives, whether they be the quest for knowledge, another publication, or a political agenda (e.g., Van Maanen, 1988).

According to Spindler and Spindler (1990), mainstream American culture is permeated by the values of independence, freedom, technological advancement, and change. These authors contend that the dominant feature of American culture is the worth placed on change. Americans are, for the most part, concerned with the future, and view change as necessary and in a positive light.

In addition, Americans value achievement, success, competition, and self-expression (Engel, 1988; Spence, 1985; Spindler & Spindler, 1990). Even when American children are very young, they are called on to express what they want before they are mature enough to do so. American parental expectations about language development and expressive capabilities are quite clear with regard to young children. Even toddlers are expected to express their needs and wants verbally and competently (Befu, 1986).

American value structures influence American fieldworkers who work with children in several ways. First, American fieldworkers seem more likely to focus on individual differences and achievements when observing and interpreting data from children's groups. Differential attention to interindividual variation as opposed to the characteristics of the whole group may result from the interaction of a fieldworker's gender with his or her cultural heritage.

For example, researchers from individualistic cultures (e.g., the United States) may be more inclined to interpret and analyze data from children's groups by placing emphasis on individual differences. By contrast, researchers from collectivist

cultures such as Japan or China may be more inclined to interpret and analyze data focusing on the characteristics of the
group at the expense of incorporating data from individual
children. Although I often focus on the group, I place more
emphasis on intraindividual and interindividual variation in
my analyses of children's cultural phenomena.

Second, American fieldworkers may be more apt to emphasize and attend selectively to changes occurring in the children's culture. The American value structure places a great deal
of emphasis on change, and change is viewed as good (Spindler
& Spindler, 1990). Studies on children's play that concentrate
on changes in group composition tend to support the notion
that American researchers value change and interpret behavior
through this value.

Third, data obtained from children's cultures are often interpreted through the values of freedom and self-reliance.
When conducting research with children, one cannot help but
notice the children who lack social skills, are dependent, and
are unable to express themselves. These are core values in
American culture, and children who are not competent in these
areas are clearly recognized.

Fourth, there is the issue of American achievement and
striving to be the best. I suspect that American fieldworkers at
times may unconsciously focus on the most popular, talented,
or sociable children because they represent the traditional, middle-class view of what children should be. For American fieldworkers, data may be interpreted using dominant, mainstream,
middle-class values. In American society, socioeconomic status
is a powerful factor that affects one's childhood and life experiences (Hunt & Prout, 1990a). This could be a particular problem when researchers from middle-class backgrounds conduct
fieldwork with children in disadvantaged neighborhoods.
Similarly, the reverse situation could give rise to misinterpretations of the children's behaviors and experiences. The socialization experiences of children, and consequently their overt

behavior, are affected by ethnicity, gender, and socioeconomic status. Thus, it seems reasonable to suppose that the bidirectional relationship between the socioeconomic status of the researcher and the children being studied will affect the interpretation of the children's behaviors.

Finally, there is the issue of language competency. I have conducted fieldwork in schools where some children are deaf and others speak English as a second language. Interpretations of children's behavior who are deaf or speak English as a second language may be misconstrued or neglected because the fieldworker has limited competency with these languages. Being fairly competent in Spanish was an advantage in schools with bilingual (Spanish and English speaking) children. I could communicate with the children in their native language and in English. Thus, I was able to establish a rapport with them, and include their experiences in my interpretations of children's cultures.

African American Culture

African American culture has its historical origins in West African cultural values and practices (Logan, 1996). It has retained traditions associated with its heritage, while incorporating elements from the assimilation with European American mainstream culture (Hale, 1986). Although ethnic minority groups in the United States share the same goals as the mainstream culture, they remain separated enough to perpetuate a distinct culture apart from mainstream America (Hale, 1986; Julian & McKenry, 1994). African Americans are one such subgroup.

One of the strongest historical legacies in the African American community is the strength and importance of the family (Franklin, 1988). For this reason, I have elected to focus on

family structure, child-rearing practices, and adult-child interactions.

One of the pervasive features of African American culture
that can be traced back to African cultural practices is the
importance of the extended family (Logan, 1996; Sudarkasa,
1988). Similar to East Indian children, African American children are often socialized in an extended family that includes
grandparents and other relatives. As Stack (1974) notes, however, in contrast to the European American community, African
Americans also use nonrelational members of the community
as important resources for child-rearing responsibilities and
socializing their children. Stack (1974) refers to these individuals as "fictive kin"—unrelated community residents who share
a strong bond and treat one another with the respect and love
equivalent to that expressed in kinship ties. This stands in
contrast to the dominant European American family organization pattern that typically includes only immediate family
members.

From a parent's perspective, the socialization process for
African American children is a difficult and problematic one.
To survive, African American children need to experience a
dual socialization process. They need to be competent members
of the black community, while simultaneously learning to function in mainstream, European American culture. Thus, parents
impart knowledge about their own culture while trying to
prepare their children for the realities of the world they will
enter (Denby & Alford, 1996; Julian & McKenry, 1994; Peters,
1988; Smith, 1996).

African American parents transmit to their children the core
American ideals of freedom, achievement, and success through
hard work. In addition, there are culture-specific values that
include unity, self-determination, collectivism, cooperative eco-
nomics, purpose, creativity, perseverance, and faith (Hale, 1991;
Logan, 1996).

Although core American ideology stresses the importance of the individual, African American children are also raised in a collectivist ideology. African American children are taught to value the connections and interdependence between and among family members. This interdependence has historical ties to West African cultural practices (Serpell, 1996), and partially explains why African Americans are viewed as people oriented rather than object oriented (Hale, 1986). As I mention in Chapter 2, "Methods: Working With Children," the African American emphasis on social interaction guides the way I conduct interviews with African American children. Although I acknowledge each child's individuality and personality, I find that African American children enjoy small-group arrangements and socializing with their peers. Thus, I frequently interview the children in small groups, and find this to be productive. I believe the children's comfort with small-group interviews is linked to the African American cultural emphasis on collectivism.

Finally, another unique feature of African American culture distinguishes it from European American culture. African American children are raised with a strong sense of faith (Hale, 1991; Smith, 1996). In the African American community, the church plays a dominant role (in concert with the family) in serving as one kind of socializing agent for children (Durodoye, 1995).

Adult notions of children reflect their prominent position in African American culture. Adults recognize that children are innately good, and children are viewed as "the centerpiece of African-American family life" (Billingsly, 1992, p. 65). Parents and children share an unconditional love, and love is never used as reinforcement for behavior (Nobles, 1988). Parents teach their children to respect authority figures, acquire a sense of obligation to the family, and have strong religious beliefs (Julian & McKenry, 1994). The way African American parents go about this is often misinterpreted by mainstream culture, however.

For example, most African American parents are quite strict with their children and use an authoritarian style of child rearing. This physical punishment is viewed as cruel when compared to the authoritative style of child rearing used by many European Americans (Denby & Alford, 1996). Some African American parents use physical punishment (accompanied by an explanation for its use to the child) to teach responsibility and obedience. Obedience is highly desirable, and viewed as a means of obtaining academic success (Denby & Alford, 1996; Peters, 1988). Recent works have attempted to use African American cultural skills to introduce alternative methods of discipline and punishment (Denby & Alford, 1996).

Fieldworkers in schools may be privy to parent-child interactions involving disciplinary actions. European American and fieldworkers from cultures that do not use physical punishment with children may interpret the parent's harshness as inappropriate, a sign of poor parenting skills, or, depending on the severity, child abuse. It is important to understand the culturally specific circumstances in which child-rearing practices emerge to interpret accurately the behaviors the fieldworker observes.

Also, fieldworkers working with children may misinterpret African American children's behaviors if they are not aware of certain cultural practices and interaction styles.[5] First, when speaking to authority figures and elders, African American children do not gaze directly into the eyes and sometimes the face of these individuals. This is often interpreted as inattentiveness on the children's part by those who are unfamiliar with this behavior. There are several viable alternative interpretations for this behavior. First, it may be disrespectful to make direct eye contact with an authority, or direct eye contact may be reserved for in-group members rather than out-group members (Hale, 1986).

Children often engage in such eye contact with their teachers. I often gauge the effectiveness of the friend role with these children by whether or not they feel comfortable exchanging eye contact with me. I have interpreted this as a sign that they do not consider me an authority figure.

African American parents are typically strict with their children. Teachers who use a permissive or inductive style often have difficulty disciplining the children and view them as unruly. The African American child, based on his or her experiences with adult authority figures, expects the teacher to be firm. This has led to misinterpretations of minority children as being misbehaved or unresponsive to adult requests. The misinterpretation is perhaps due in part to miscommunication between the child and teacher based on the child and teacher's cultural expectations of adult-child interactions.

Finally, African American children tend to be more active and physical than European American children. This high degree of physical movement is often misinterpreted as hyperactivity or an inability to sit patiently and pay attention in class. Motor activity, performance, and creative expression are all intricately linked for African American children (Hale, 1986).

East Indian Culture

There are only a few contemporary societies in which cultural, religious, and social practices have withstood change or westernization. India is one such country where traditions have remained remarkably stable for centuries. It is united by Hinduism and the caste system, and the traditional extended family persists in spite of urbanization and the increase in nuclear families (Roopnarine, Talukder, Jain, Joshi, & Srivastav, 1990). Thus, the majority of East Indian children spend their formative years as members of joint and extended families. Parents, grandparents, and aunts and uncles each play a role in a child's socialization (Roopnarine & Hossain, 1992; Roopnarine, Hossain, Gill, & Brophy, 1994; Roopnarine et al., 1990).

Social and religious factors guide a society's views of children and childhood. In India, the caste system dictates one's childhood experiences, and Hindu doctrine guides and influences child-rearing practices (Roopnarine & Hossain, 1992; Roopnarine, Hossain et al., 1994). One important socialization experience involves the differential position of sons and daughters. According to religious doctrine and cultural ideology, sons are desirable and preferable to daughters. The eldest son holds a respected position in the family (Roopnarine et al., 1990; Suppal, Roopnarine, Buesig, & Bennet, 1996). Sons fulfill religious obligations in sacraments and perpetuate their family's name and legacy. Daughters are viewed as burdensome, a consequence of the dowry marriage practice.

Finally, ideological beliefs govern the roles of men and women in Indian society. Such views are deeply rooted in historical sacred texts and religious doctrine. For example, Indian society can best be characterized as patriarchal and authoritarian. In general, men occupy positions of respect and power; women are viewed as subservient to men in marriage, and status is achieved after bearing children (Roopnarine & Hossain, 1992; Suppal et al., 1996).

Such views influence child-rearing and parental responsibilities. A dichotomy exists in traditional Indian family practices—women are associated with the home and physical care of children, whereas fathers are associated with the economic viability of the household. Thus, mothers are the primary caretakers of children and share a close, intimate bond with their children. By contrast, Indian fathers are depicted as feared and stern parents who participate in few child care responsibilities (Roopnarine & Hossain, 1992; Suppal et al., 1996).

Parent-infant play, particularly between Indian fathers and infants, does not involve the rough or physical play observed in American society (Roopnarine et al., 1990). Parent-infant interactions in India contain a great deal of holding, cuddling, and tactile stimulation that reflect cultural values of calmness and tranquillity (Roopnarine, Hossain et al., 1994). In addition, Indian mothers are more likely to follow a child's inclinations rather than direct the child's behavior. This stems from a belief that the child possesses certain innate capabilities that should be respected (Kakar, 1978, cited in Roopnarine & Hossain, 1992).

Indian researchers working with American children may focus their observations on behaviors consistent with Indian culture and child-rearing practices. Thus, American parents' rough physical play with their infants could be misconstrued if interpreted through Indian value structures. One could reasonably argue that these experiences will color the East Indian researcher's interpretations of American children and vice versa.

Conversely, American researchers studying child behavior in Indian society may not be cognizant of the importance of the extended family in a child's socialization, and may rely on American household forms (i.e., the nuclear and single-parent families) to interpret Indian behavior. Misinterpretations of data may arise when American concepts of household forms, socialization, and child rearing are transposed onto the Indian data. For example, the extended family has never really been a part of European American culture (Hareven, 1992), and American fieldworkers may have difficulty interpreting a parent's role in the socialization of their children. American fieldworkers might focus only on parent-child interactions, as would be appropriate for American culture, and overlook the importance of other relational ties in the child's development.

In Indian society, the caste system determines one's childhood experiences. American fieldworkers working with children are accustomed to focusing on the factors of race, ethnicity, and socioeconomic status when interpreting data on children's cultures. Thus, it might be difficult for American fieldworkers to incorporate the influence of the caste system in interpreting field data on children. Finally, American society is as diverse in its religious sects as it is in ethnic groups. No one religious tenet defines American ideology. Thus, American fieldworkers may overlook the importance of religious beliefs when interpreting children's experiences.

Japanese Culture

Japan is one of the few industrial societies in which traditional cultural values still survive. For the most part, Japan has escaped Western influence partially because it has been welcoming foreign visitors for less than a century (Stevenson et al., 1986).

Since the 8th century, Japanese philosophy has regarded the child as a "jewel" (Takeuchi, 1994). This notion arose as a consequence of religious beliefs and economic factors. Yamamura (1986, p. 30) provides an explanation for the existence of this metaphor. Japanese parents are said to become so strongly attached to their children that they become "lost." According to Buddhist tenets, this love is contaminated with earthly desire—*kobonno*. This emotionality is coupled with the knowledge that one's children will eventually accept fiscal responsibility for their parents and family. Thus, religious and economic factors have led to conceiving of children as jewels.

The period of childhood is viewed positively in Japanese ideology. Childhood and the quality of childishness do not carry negative connotations (Chen, 1996). This stands in contrast to American views of childhood. According to Goodwin (1997), children's life experiences are rarely researched because childhood is viewed as a stage in the socialization process through which children must pass en route to the final desirable product, a culturally competent adult.

Japanese fieldworkers guided by their own cultural notions of children most likely view children as inherently good. In fact, in Japan, children are viewed as pure and noble. Adults in general and parents in particular, as a consequence of their adult status, are perceived as insignificant. In Japanese ideology, children are viewed as superior to adults (Yamamura, 1986). Japanese fieldworkers may be inclined to indulge and over-protect the children they study as a consequence of Japanese historical views.

Because children are perceived as superior to adults in Japan, such notions could also influence the researcher-subject relationship Japanese fieldworkers establish with their young subjects insofar as the fieldworkers may be inclined to revere child participants. In their field interactions with children, Japanese fieldworkers may unconsciously adjust their behavior so that the balance of power in this relationship is tipped in the children's favor. Such interactional styles may lead to reverence of one's participants. The reverence of children in Japanese society may lead to the study of children at the expense of studying adult populations.

In Japanese culture, emphasis is placed on interpersonal relationships. The self is defined by one's relationship to others (Triandis, 1989). Members of Japanese society are interconnected, and these interconnections are maintained through acts of debt and gratitude. Depending on one's relationship to another person, refusal to assist him or her when he or she is in need may be considered disgraceful. Such cultural prescriptions for behavior intensify a child's already existing familial obligation to care for his or her parents (Befu, 1986).

In American culture, the self is defined by individual characteristics and goals. Japanese notions of parental care neither exist in American culture nor can be transported into other cultures due to a variety of social, cultural, and economic factors. The emphasis placed on interpersonal dependence in Japanese culture stands in direct contrast to American cultural values. In our society, individuals are concerned with what is in their own best interests, and a person could easily refuse a relative's or stranger's request for assistance with little or no repercussions (e.g., Befu, 1986; Engel, 1988; Spence, 1985). In addition, American patterns of marriage and residence and postmodern family structures often do not include the intense familial obligations found in collectivist cultures. In American society, it is not uncommon for grown children to place their aging parents in nursing homes in the care of unrelated professionals rather than accept responsibility and provide care for their parents at home.

Unlike western conceptions of children and childhood, Japanese cultural conceptions of children have remained remarkably stable throughout history. Japanese children, unlike their western peers, pass through socially approved age-graded stages in their transition from child to adult status. This transitional process has been preserved since historical time (Yamamura, 1986). Children were and are viewed as objects of adult love, and today still occupy a central place in Japanese society. Contemporary Japanese children are overprotected and indulged by their parents—remnants of historical beliefs about children (Takeuchi, 1994; Yamamura, 1986).

For example, Chen (1996) comments on how visitors to Japan cannot help but notice how indulgent adults are with children. According to western notions of parent-child interactions, Japanese children are spoiled. Japanese children and their parents share an incredibly close bond, however, and Japanese children are particularly well behaved.

Adult indulgence of children is linked to cultural conceptions of children and parental views of children's behaviors. For example, Japanese parents believe that children should not be left alone, and that someone should always be with them. The parental desire to prevent loneliness in children is the reasoning behind the cultural practice of cobathing and sleeping with children—times when children are likely to confront loneliness.

A third situation in which loneliness may arise involves separation of a caregiver. Hence, baby-sitting is rarely practiced, and this serves to intensify the already close bond between mother and child. Such cultural practices meet children's emotional needs (Chen, 1996).

Japan is a collectivist culture (Kashima, Yamaguchi, & Kim, 1995; Triandis, 1989; Wagner, 1995). In Japanese society, emphasis is placed on fulfilling the needs and goals of the group above one's own needs. Individual independence is also recognized within the group, however. Japanese society values obedience, conformity, group harmony, cooperation, self-confidence, ambiguity in self-expression, and putting forth one's best effort (Azuma, 1986; Befu, 1986; Tobin et al., 1989).

For Japanese parents, *amae* (translated roughly as dependence) is a desirable quality in children. The ultimate goal in the socialization process is to produce a mature adult—one who is "dependent in a sophisticated manner" (Chen, 1996, p. 123). These individuals know when and how to produce culturally appropriate responses and can anticipate and meet the needs of others.

In most western societies, particularly in American society, individualism is the pervading cultural ideology (Engel, 1988; Spence, 1985; Spindler & Spindler, 1983). In fact, American cultural values are the antithesis of Japanese values. Americans encourage their children to seek autonomy rather than maternal dependence, expect directness in social interaction, and strive for self-initiative, free will, and uniqueness (Azuma, 1986; Befu, 1986). In American society, decision making is an individual process, and even young children are socialized to make their own decisions, often before they are capable of doing so (Befu, 1986).

In social interaction, Japanese adults rarely express their feelings clearly in front of children. More important, adults do not express positive emotions in front of children because adults presumably lack the confidence that the divine child possesses. Rather, adults primarily express the emotions of guilt or shame in front of children (Yamamura, 1986). Such communication and interactive styles may affect the ease with which Japanese fieldworkers establish rapport with children from cultures other than their own. For example, young American children often evaluate a person's demeanor and desire to be with them by facial expressions. Smiles are associated with people who are "nice," whereas frowns are associated with people who are "mean."

Given the emphasis placed on collectivism, it seems reasonable to suppose that Japanese researchers may have a tacit inclination to focus only on group behavior when studying children, rather than looking at the play behavior of individual children. Thus, for example, when studying children's play, Japanese researchers may be more inclined to concentrate on group play rather than on solitary or parallel play. Consequently, their interpretations and analyses of data on children's cultures may place more emphasis on the group, rather than addressing intraindividual and interindividual nuances of behavior. Also, in Japanese society, there is a cultural avoidance of criticizing others. Children are encouraged to seek *hansei*—self-examination (White & LeVine, 1986, p. 59).

In American children, criticism of others, whether about how well one plays or particular behaviors one is performing, is commonplace. Japanese fieldworkers may have difficulty dealing with or interpreting American children's critical nature. Japanese fieldworkers could find it difficult to displace their own cultural notions when it comes to interpreting data on children's behaviors from other cultures.

Finally, Japanese cultural behavior may affect the interview process with children. In my own fieldwork with children, I rely heavily on unstructured and informal interviewing. American children are accustomed to respond to adult queries, and do so without much resistance. Japanese children, however, depending on the contextual situation, may interpret adult queries as a signal that they have misbehaved. In fact, nursery school teachers in Japan often employ innocent questions as a form of discipline (Lewis, 1986). Japanese fieldworkers may be reluctant to query young children because of the manner in which adult queries form children's responses in Japan.

An advantage in fieldwork with children may be the way Japanese parents address their children. For example, parents typically refer to one another by the terms "mother" and "father"—especially when children are present. This is in contrast to terms of address used by western parents, which typically include the use of first names. Japanese parents often "pretend to be children" to anticipate children's needs, and in terms of address, take on the child's point of view of the relationship (Chen, 1996, p. 125). This desire to take on the child's point of view is the essence of participant observation with children, in which the fieldworker wishes to present the children's experiences in their own terms. The desire to take on the children's point of view is the foundation of Japanese socialization (Chen, 1996).

A final example from Tobin et al.'s (1989) cross-cultural comparison of preschools in Japan, China, and the United States should illuminate the difficulty in interpreting behavior from different cultures using emic value constructs and practices. As part of the method for this study, the authors employed visual ethnography. Taped sessions from each school were shown to teachers from all three cultures in the sample. Each teacher was then asked to evaluate the classroom management techniques employed. In all cases, teachers responded to and evaluated the target teacher's behavior based on their own cultural ideologies about child behavior, classroom management, and societal values.

In one taped classroom scenario, a Japanese teacher provides absolutely no direction when one child is misbehaving and other children complain about his behavior to the teacher. Instead of resolving the conflict for them, the teacher tells the children it is their problem, and they must resolve how to deal with the disruptive student. In Japan, nursery school teachers seldom intervene in children's affairs. Rather, they typically encourage children to manage and resolve their own problems (see also Lewis, 1986).

When asked to evaluate this episode, the American teachers found the Japanese teacher's lack of direction inappropriate for the classroom because they were judging her behavior based on American concepts and prescriptions of teacher behavior in classroom management issues. American teachers manage children's conflicts for them, and American values of individualism could not be transported into the Japanese classroom and into a society that values collectivism, group cooperation, and obedience from its members (see also Lewis, 1986).

The issues addressed in the previous examples involve the concepts of cultural relativism and ethnocentrism. Cross-cultural psychology and cross-cultural research seek to examine and compare human behavior across cultures to search for culture-specific and cultural universals of behavior (Segall et al., 1990). Fieldworkers working with children need to be aware of their own cultural biases, notions, and practices when interpreting children's behavior from cultures other than their own.

How Researchers Represent Children

Research orientations and theoretical perspectives are also pervasive factors that can influence fieldworkers' interpretations of children's cultures (Sutton-Smith, 1994; Van Maanen, 1988). Although these factors exert their own influence on the research, they are often entwined with a fieldworker's gender and ethnicity.

In a recent work, Schwartzman (1995) revisits her analysis of how researchers represent children and how these conceptions of children affect the fieldworker's descriptions and interpretations of children's cultures. In the first anthropological work to address children's play, Schwartzman (1978) identifies several metaphors that served to guide researchers' views on childhood and child socialization. The following discussion is a summary of her metaphorical analogues that influence the interpretations of children's cultures. Bear in mind that these are primarily western notions, and that metaphors for children vary cross-culturally (see Hwang et al., 1996, for a discussion of cultural-specific images of childhood).

Children as Primitive

The view of children as primitive was predominant in studies conducted in the 19th and early 20th centuries, and the effect of evolutionary theory on child development is clearly evident. The stage theories of Freud (1900, 1905), Erikson (1963, 1968), and Piaget (1929, 1959, 1963) are testimony to the influence evolutionary thought had on child development. Stanley Hall's capitulation theory of play (see Hughes, 1995) sees forms of human play as remnants of our evolutionary past. For example, an infant crawling on all fours is viewed as a reflection of our evolutionary history before humans were bipedal. This is reflected in contemporary researchers, who view children as immature and incomplete because the end product of development is a fully formed adult. Goodwin (1997) argues that the prevailing western view of the socialization processes of children and childhood as inferior to adulthood has led to obscurity in anthropological research.

Children as Copycats

The view of children as copycats of adults was popular in the early 20th century. Children were conceived of as passive imitators of adult behavior. Groos's (1901) theory of play as practice for adult skills typifies this notion. Researchers influenced by this metaphor view children's play as a means by which children rehearse skills that will prepare them for adult life. Psychological theories such as behaviorism contributed to the view that humans are passive organisms. The notion that children can invent or create their own culture or behaviors eventually displaced this view.

Children as Personality Trainees

The view of children as personality trainees has spanned much of the 20th century and is currently popular with psychological anthropologists who study the relationship between culture and personality. This view emerged historically with Benedict's (1934) contention that cultures possess a single, dominant pattern, and this pattern is linked to modal personality types. Although Benedict worked with adult communities, Mead (1961) searched for the link between the influence of culture on adolescent life experiences and personality types. Researchers who adopt this view often fail to take into account inter- and intraindividual variations in personality. In addition, this view lends itself to viewing children's behavior in a vacuum rather than recognizing the integrative nature of culture (Harkness, 1996). The importance of context in interpreting children's cultures is addressed by Graue and Walsh (in press).

Children as Monkeys

The view of children as monkeys is popular among child ethologists, who believe that human behavior can be examined via the same methods employed for studying the behavior of animal species (e.g., McGrew, 1972). The use of ethograms to study children's behavior emerged in the 1970s, and is used in contemporary research in children's play, particularly aggressive play. Researchers who use this metaphor typically focus on overt behaviors and study sequential patterns of behavior.

Children as Critics

In this view, "children act as interpreters, commentators, and even critics of their own as well as adults' activities" (Schwartzman, 1978, p. 25). This view is reflected in the study of children's verbal art forms in which children often extract some of their material from the adult world in an effort to make sense of it. Children are viewed as active actors in their social world.

Schwartzman (1978, 1995) argues that these metaphors are linked to the theoretical stance taken by the fieldworker, and these ultimately influence the way the fieldworker views and writes about children's cultures. Similarly, Sutton-Smith (cited in Brown, 1995, p. 36) notes that western metaphors of childhood (e.g., the child of God, the child as future, and the imaginary child) also promote different views about childhood and how it is interpreted.

One's research orientation also guides the direction of the fieldwork process. Anthropologists, sociologists, psychologists, educators, linguists, health professionals, and others all engage in qualitative research with children. Each is trained to interpret behaviors and experiences from a particular vantage point, however. Sometimes these vantage points overlap between disciplines; at other times, these vantage points are disparate.

Even in the same discipline, disagreements among interpretations of children's behavior occur. A clinical psychologist and evolutionary psychologist would surely have different views about why babies cry. Similarly, a psychological anthropologist and physical anthropologist may disagree about interpretations of children's play behaviors. The psychological anthropologist might emphasize the role of culture in interpreting children's behaviors. In contrast, the physical anthropologist might view the children's behavior from an ethological perspective. In either case, interpretations reflect the researcher's training.

Notes

1. The term *race* is an arbitrary construct whose cultural and biological meanings and applications are imprecise. I use *ethnicity* in the text to refer to membership in a particular ethnic group. This group comprises individuals who share a common language and participate in a common cultural value ideology (Barth, 1992).

2. America is a culturally diverse society. The term *American culture* can neither accurately define nor do justice to our cultural diversity and numerous ethnic groups. American culture when employed in this text refers to mainstream European American culture (Spindler & Spindler, 1990).

3. Other factors have influenced the movement of play from outdoors on the playgrounds and in the neighborhood to indoor facilities. Such factors include safety issues, the wide appeal of video games, and the lack of spontaneous outdoor play by contemporary children (Rivkin, 1995).

4. Recent authors (e.g., Lynott & Logue, 1993) have argued that those who claim there are hurried children have failed to take into account the diverse life experiences of American children. Further claims of the hurried child have not examined the connection between this condition and factors such as age, gender, and race. Lynott and Logue (1993) argue that the majority of American children may not experience this notion of the hurried child. Experiences of childhood are dependent on many factors, including race, gender, class, and locale (Berrol, 1985; Hunt & Prout, 1990b).

5. I learned a great deal of information about African American adult-child interactions from the children's grandmothers and parents (see also Hale, 1991).

CHAPTER 6

Concluding Remarks

Contributions to the reflexive nature of fieldwork (e.g., Bell et al., 1993; Kleinman & Copp, 1993; Kulick & Wilson, 1995) share a common theme, that is, they acknowledge that fieldwork does not take place in a vacuum. Rather, it is an interpretive process guided by a variety of factors such as the fieldworker's personal traits, research orientation, and theoretical perspectives (e.g., Agar, 1986/1995; Allum, 1991; Bell et al., 1993; Bishop, 1991; Van Maanen, 1988, 1995).

In this work, I have attempted to demonstrate that the fieldworker's personal traits (i.e., gender and ethnicity) play a role in guiding and assisting the fieldwork process with children. The bearing that these factors have on the interpretive process has been documented for adult communities (e.g., Bell et al., 1993; Warren, 1988; Whitehead & Conaway, 1986; D. Wolf, 1996a). Such issues are rarely explored in the fieldwork process with children, however.

Gender is a classificational construct that children (and grown-ups) often employ to make sense out of their social world. For example, the fieldworker's gender influences interpersonal dynamics when establishing relationships with children and school personnel. Field relationships with children constantly change through the negotiation and renegotiation of roles applied to the fieldworker (Warren, 1988), and the fieldworker's gender may facilitate the rapport he or she establishes with the children. Some children view a female fieldworker as nurturant because she shares gender membership with the category "mother." Because mother is a female and nurturing, these qualities are extended to the female fieldworker, and she is sometimes approached when the children need to be comforted. Thus, she is able to establish a trusting relationship with the children in a variety of contexts and research roles (e.g., friend, classmate, and nurturing grown-up). Each construction and reconstruction of the fieldworker's gender is dictated by the contextualized aspects of interactions with the children.

Some children's perceptions and categorization of male fieldworkers may not emphasize nurturing qualities, and the children might not seek male fieldworkers for comfort. Male fieldworkers might be able to capitalize on displaying nurturing behaviors in addition to their own interaction styles to extend the contexts of their interactions with the children.

The fieldworker's gender affects the fieldwork process in other ways. For example, although teaching is primarily a female-dominated vocation, there is a clear distinction between positions occupied by females and males within this field. Males typically hold administrative positions, whereas females usually teach children in the younger grades (Allan, 1993; Kauppinen-Toropainen & Lammi, 1993). This division of labor influences the relationships the fieldworker is able to establish with school personnel. For example, on his first visits in an elementary school, Norris Johnson (1986) experienced some friction from the female teachers. They linked him to the principal and male administrative power simply because Johnson and the principal shared gender membership. As a female fieldworker, I shared gender membership, vocational experiences, and certain life experiences with the female teachers with whom I have worked. These connections helped me establish a rapport with the teachers, who are vital in allowing the fieldworker the time to pursue his or her goals. This would presumably hold true for male fieldworkers establishing relationships with male teachers.

Gender also influences one's ability to move freely through the schools, and can constrain or limit one's interactions with children. Legitimate roles fulfilled by females on school premises are teachers, staff, or one of the children's mothers. Because I was female and the approximate age of most of the women in the school, school personnel and other visiting adults (who did not have any contact with me) presumed I must have been fulfilling one of the roles mentioned previously.

Traveling unrestrained through school areas would not be so easily accomplished by male fieldworkers. Teachers of young children are not usually males (Cohen, 1990; Kauppinen-Toropainen & Lammi, 1993), and their presence would not be easily explained because American fathers infrequently visit their children during school hours.

Gender also influences what cultural phenomena will be observed, how data are collected, and how children's behavior is interpreted. The notion that male and female fieldworkers attend selectively to different aspects of the same culture has been documented clearly in adult communities (e.g., Dwyer, 1978; Dwyer, 1982; Murphy & Murphy, 1974, 1985). This principle also operates when observing children's cultures.

The childhood socialization experiences of adult male and female fieldworkers may influence what children's behaviors they attend to and how they interpret them. Research suggests that rough-and-tumble play cross-culturally is the dominion of boys, and it is a topic studied predominantly by male researchers (e.g., Goldstein, 1996; Pellegrini, 1996). It seems likely that female fieldworkers would not concentrate on this behavior due to inadequate play experiences as children, cultural conditioning that views rough-and-tumble play as inappropriate for girls, and no desire to participate in or observe this aspect of children's cultures. Connor (1989) clearly supports the idea that men and women (and children) differentially interpret episodes of rough-and-tumble play. Women tend to interpret rough-and-tumble play as real aggression, whereas men, based on their prior play experiences, do not. Prior play experiences appear to determine whether one can distinguish between playful and real aggression.

Gender as it is linked to socialization experiences also influences a fieldworker's ability to participate in the children's culture. Androgynous fieldworkers working with children would likely have a distinct advantage over stereotypical feminine and masculine ones. I was able to participate in a wide range of activities due to my own play experiences as a child. I was equally familiar and comfortable with the boys' and girls' play activities, and became a desirable playmate in part because of my play competencies. Male fieldworkers, who are socialized more intensely as children with respect to sex-typed behavior (e.g., Robinson & Morris, 1986; Tracy, 1987), may not have had any experience with opposite-sex play, particularly sedentary pretend play such as house or baby. Integration into such play activities might be difficult, or the fieldworker might opt not to study these kinds of activities. This situation parallels female fieldworkers' difficulties in studying rough-and-tumble play. Prior to fieldwork, some female fieldworkers may wish to become more familiar with or experience more physical kinds of play. In contrast, some male fieldworkers may wish to participate in or experience girls' games of pretend.

Gender also influences one's method of data collection and interpretation of children's behavior. I do not believe that the way men and women ethnographers go about their business is related to innate differences between men and women, however. Rather, I believe that the differential socialization experiences of men and women can account for the different perspectives that arise in the fieldwork process (e.g., Bronfenbrenner, 1979b, 1986, 1989).

For example, it seems likely that female researchers are more attuned to individual differences and interindividual variation that male researchers are (Fedigan & Fedigan, 1989). I do not believe this is due to a woman's innate sense of detail, but that it is a consequence of socialization experiences. Women are socialized to participate in dyadic relationships, whereas men's socialization experiences emphasize the group (e.g., Collins, 1984; Maccoby, 1990). Thus, it seems logical that female researchers place more emphasis on individuals and interindividual variation.

Socialization experiences can provide an explanation for why women fieldworkers tend to focus on specific relationships and social connections rather than concentrating exclusively on the individual. A case in point is the differential perspectives of Stack (1974) and Liebow (1967), both of whom studied African American communities. Stack's ethnography on African American families reveals the richness of social networks and familial connections that exist in her community via subjects' feelings. By contrast, Liebow concentrates on the men who occupy the street corner, paying little attention to the other relationships that exist in their lives.

The influence of a fieldworker's ethnicity on the process with adults has recently been brought to light (e.g., Bell et al., 1993; Pederson, 1993; Van Maanen, 1995). Fieldworkers enter the field with their own emic preexpectations of behavior and cognitive categories that can have a bearing on the fieldwork process. The issue should not be reduced to the insider-outsider debate, however. In agreement with most researchers, I believe that a fieldworker's ethnicity should not preclude his or her ability to produce an accurate interpretation of a group. Rather, fieldworkers should recognize that certain aspects of their cultural heritage may tacitly or overtly guide how they go about the interpretive process.

The fieldworker's ethnicity can influence several aspects of the fieldwork process with children. First, ideas of children and childhood are emic constructs, and such conceptions influence the way researchers view and interpret children's behaviors and interact with them. Thus, fieldworkers from different cultures enter the field with different preexpectations of children and their behaviors. These come into play during the interpretive stage of fieldwork.

Second, cultural ideology (e.g., aspects of the macrosystem) exerts an influence on certain aspects of the fieldwork process. If one employs the continuum of collectivism-individualism to classify societies, American culture is an individualistic one. Core values in our society are achievement, freedom, competitiveness, self-expression, and independence (e.g., Engel, 1988; Triandis et al., 1988). An individual's pursuits are given priority compared to those of the group. Fieldworkers from individualistic cultures may be inclined to focus on children's interpersonal interactions rather than group structure. Conversely, fieldworkers raised with a collectivist ideology may attend more to the group and not incorporate the experiences of individual children.

The cultural diversity in the United States becomes a factor when conducting fieldwork with children. American fieldworkers primarily receive their training in western schools and adopt western theoretical vantage points. The extension of European American middle-class values to all ethnic minority groups in the United States is problematic. Although these groups share mainstream American values, they simultaneously transmit distinct cultural practices to their children (Julian & McKenry, 1994). Consider the status of African American children, who undergo dual socialization processes so that they can function in their own and the mainstream culture (Hale, 1986; Logan, 1996).

European American and fieldworkers from other cultures may not be familiar with the subtleties of African American communication styles, and consequently may misinterpret children's behaviors because of this. For example, interviewing African American children in a group appears to complement the emphasis placed on social interaction in the African American community. This knowledge is beneficial because it helps the researcher select a methodology that is compatible with the children's experiences. Also, certain nonverbal communication patterns are unique to African American culture and are not shared by European American culture. Such patterns are often more difficult to learn than language and may be passed over by the fieldworker.

One example is eye contact with out-group members. Some African American children are socialized not to make direct eye contact with an authority figure. Teachers who do not share the children's ethnic heritage often interpret this behavior as a sign of inattentiveness. Other examples include misinterpretations of the children's motor activity, responses to the teacher's disciplinary styles, and parenting behaviors. Such knowledge would be beneficial for fieldworkers because it would help them interpret the children's experiences.

Examples from East Indian culture such as family structure and parent-child play interactions demonstrate how the culture in which one is raised affects fieldwork with children. For example, the East Indian practice of socializing children within extended families illustrates the difficulty in applying emic concepts to behaviors observed in other cultures. American and other fieldworkers raised in societies where the nuclear family is the norm may overlook the importance of other individuals as socializing agents for children.

Similarly, examples from Japanese culture illustrate how cultural beliefs and emic conceptions of children may guide

how Japanese fieldworkers view children's behaviors from
different cultures. These include collectivist beliefs, Japanese
interaction patterns between children and adults, and the idea
that children are viewed as divine. Culturally specific adult-
child interaction styles may influence the success a fieldworker
has with establishing a rapport with the children.

Japanese adults do not typically reveal their feelings to
children. More important, adults do not display positive emotions in front of children because adults do not possess the
conviction the divine child does. Such practices may hinder the
rapport the fieldworker is able to establish with the children.
American children often use facial expressions and the expression of emotion to evaluate whether a person is "nice" or
"mean." Failure to display emotions in front of children may
affect the fieldworker's ability to establish field relationships
with them.

Some cultural practices may also facilitate fieldwork with
children. Consider the terms of address employed by Japanese
adults. They address one another as "mother" or "father"—especially when children are present. These terms are employed
to emphasize the child's vantage point in the relationship
(Chen, 1996). This emphasis on viewing the world from a child's
perspective is the hallmark of Japanese socialization, and the
goal of fieldworkers who wish to understand children's cultures from their perspective. This stands in contrast to many
western societies where adults are addressed by a first name
rather than a social category.

One's microsystem also influences how one perceives and
interprets children's behaviors. For example, American fieldworkers raised in modern or postmodern families enter the
field with different preexpectations of children and notions of
childhood. Experiences of childhood (as in other cultures) are
also entwined with a variety of other factors such as religious
beliefs and socioeconomic status. Hence, American ideology
is often associated with mainstream, middle-class American

values, even though individual American children have disparate childhood experiences (Hunt & Prout, 1990a, 1990b).

In addition, the microsystem and macrosystem do not function as separate entities. Rather, each level blends into the other, and there is reciprocal influence and interaction between them.

This book is a preliminary exploration of how a researcher's personal traits can affect the fieldwork process with children. Certainly not all issues are addressed, and some are addressed only peripherally. I hope this work stimulates conversation on these issues and encourages fieldworkers who work with children (and adults) to explore the factors that affect this process.

References

Abramson, A. (1993). Between autobiography and method: Being male, seeing myth and the analysis of structures of gender and sexuality in the eastern interior of Fiji. In D. Bell, P. Caplan, & W. Karim (Eds.), *Gendered fields: Women, men and ethnography* (pp. 63-77). London: Routledge.

Abu-Lughod, L. (1992). *Writing women's worlds*. Berkeley, CA: University of California Press.

Agar, M. (1973). *Ripping and running: A formal ethnography of urban heroin addicts*. New York: Seminar.

Agar, M. (1980). *The professional stranger*. New York: Holt, Rinehart & Winston.

Agar, M. (1995). *Speaking of ethnography* (Qualitative Research Methods Series Vol. 2, 8th ed.). Newbury Park, CA: Sage. (Original work published in 1986)

Ahmed, M. (1983). Important questions on non-formal education. *Perspectives, 13,* 37-47.

123

Alasuutari, P. (1995). *Researching culture: Qualitative method and cultural studies.* Newbury Park, CA: Sage.

Allan, J. (1993). Male elementary teachers: Experiences and perspectives. In C. Williams (Ed.), *Doing "women's work": Men in nontraditional occupations* (pp. 113-127). Newbury Park, CA: Sage.

Allen, R. (1991). *Singing in the spirit.* Philadelphia: University of Pennsylvania Press.

Allum, K. (1991). *On conducting educational research in the field: The evolution on an ethnographic experience from passive to active to participant observation.* (ERIC Document Reproduction Service No. ED 334224)

Almquist, B. (1989). Age and gender differences in children's Christmas requests. *Play & Culture, 2,* 2-19.

Ambert, A. (1994). A qualitative study of peer abuse and its effects: Theoretical and empirical implications. *Journal of Marriage and Family, 56,* 119-131.

Andereck, M. (1992). *Ethnic awareness and the school* (Series on Race and Ethnic Relations, Vol. 5). Newbury Park, CA: Sage.

Anderson, C. (1981). Parent-child relationships: A context for reciprocal developmental influence. *Counselling Psychologist, 9,* 35-44.

Aptekar, L. (1988). *Street children of Cali.* Durham, NC: Duke University Press.

Argyle, M., & Henderson, M. (1984). The rules of friendship. *Journal of Personal and Social Relationships, 1,* 211-237.

Aries, P. (1962). *Centuries of childhood: A social history of family life.* New York: Vintage.

Asher, S., & Gottman, J. (Eds.). (1981). *The development of children's friendships.* Cambridge, UK: Cambridge University Press.

Ashby, L. (1985). Partial promises and semi-visible youths: The Depression and World War II. In J. Hawes & N. Hiner (Eds.), *American childhood: A research guide and historical handbook* (pp. 489-532). Westport, CT: Greenwood.

Axinn, W. (1991). The influence of interviewer sex on response to sensitive questions in Nepal. *Social Science Research, 20,* 303-318.

Azuma, H. (1986). Why study child development in Japan. In H. Stevenson, H. Azuma, & H. Hakuta (Eds.), *Child development and education in Japan* (pp. 3-12). New York: Freeman.

Back, L. (1993). Masculinity and fieldwork in a south London adolescent community. In D. Bell, P. Caplan, & W. Karim (Eds.), *Gendered fields: Women, men & ethnography* (pp. 215-233). London: Routledge.

Bandura, A. (1977). *Social learning theory.* Englewood Cliffs, NJ: Prentice Hall.

Barth, F. (1992, November). *Ethnic groups and boundaries: The social organization of cultural difference.* Lecture delivered at the 90th annual meeting of the American Anthropological Association, Chicago.

Bateson, G. (1956). *Steps to an ecology of mind.* New York: Penguin.

Beales, R. (1985). The child in seventeenth-century America. In J. Hawes & N. Hiner (Eds.), *American childhood: A research guide and historical handbook* (pp. 15-54). Westport, CT: Greenwood.

Befu, H. (1986). The social and cultural background of child development in Japan and the United States. In H. Stevenson, H. Azuma, & K. Hakuta (Eds.), *Child development and education in Japan* (pp. 28-38). New York: Freeman.

Bell, D. (1993). Introduction 1: The context. In D. Bell, P. Caplan, & W. Karim (Eds.), *Gendered fields: Women, men & ethnography* (pp. 1-18). London: Routledge.

Bell, D., Caplan, P., & Karim, W. (Eds.). (1993). *Gendered fields: Women, men & ethnography.* London: Routledge.

Bem, S. (1981). Gender schema theory: A cognitive account of sex typing. *Psychological Review, 88,* 354-364.

Bem, S. (1983). Gender schema theory and its implications for child development: Raising gender-aschematic children in a gender-schematic society. *Signs, 8,* 598-616.

Bem, S. (1985). Androgyny and gender schema theory: A conceptual and empirical integration. In T. Sonderegger (Ed.), *Nebraska symposium on motivation, 1984: Psychology and gender.* Lincoln: University of Nebraska Press.

Bem, S. (1993). *The lenses of gender.* Cambridge, MA: Harvard University Press.

Benedict, R. (1934). *Patterns of culture.* New York: Mentor.

Beoku-Betts, J. (1994). When black is not enough: Doing field research among Gullah women. *NWSA Journal, 6,* 413-433.

Berger, R. (1993). From text to (field)work and back again: Theorizing a post(modern) ethnography. *Anthropological Quarterly, 66,* 174-186.

Berik, G. (1996). Understanding the gender system in Turkey: Fieldwork dilemmas of conformity and intervention. In D. Wolf (Ed.), *Feminist dilemmas in fieldwork* (pp. 56-71). Boulder, CO: Westview.

Bernard, H. (1994). *Research methods in anthropology.* Thousand Oaks, CA: Sage.

Bernheimer, L. (1986). The use of qualitative methodology in child health research. *Children's Health Care, 14,* 224-232.

Berrol, S. (1985). Ethnicity and American children. In J. Hawes & N. Hiner (Eds.), *American childhood: A research guide and historical handbook* (pp. 343-376). Westport, CT: Greenwood.

Billingsly, A. (1992). *Climbing Jacob's ladder: The enduring legacy of African-American families.* New York: Simon & Schuster.

Birth, K. (1990). The reading and writing of ethnographies. *American Ethnologist, 17,* 549-557.

Bishop, W. (1991). *Reliable and valid stories?—Turning ethnographic data into narratives.* (ERIC Document Reproduction Service No. ED 331048)

Bleier, R. (1984). *Science and gender: A critique of biology and its theories on women.* New York: Pergamon.

Block, J. (1983). Differential premises arising from differential socialization of the sexes: Some conjectures. *Child Development, 54,* 1335-1354.

Boros, A. (1988). Being subjective as a sociologist. *Journal of Applied Sociology, 5,* 15-31.

Boxwell, D. (1992). "Sis Cat" as ethnographer: Self-presentation and self-inscription in Zora Neale Hurston's "Mules and Men." *African American Review, 26,* 605-618.

Boyden, J. (1990). Childhood and the policy makers: A comparative perspective on the globalization of childhood. In A. Hunt & J. Prout (Eds.), *Constructing and reconstructing childhood* (pp. 184-215). Bristol, PA: Falmer.

Bredekamp, S. (Ed.). (1987). *Developmentally appropriate practice in early childhood programs serving children from birth through age eight.* Washington, DC: National Association for the Education of Young Children.

Bredekamp, S., & Rosegrant, T. (Eds.). (1992). *Reaching potentials: Appropriate curriculum and assessment for young children.* Washington, DC: National Association for the Education of Young Children.

Briggs, J. (1986). Kapluna daughter. In P. Golde (Ed.), *Women in the field: Anthropological experiences* (pp. 19-46). Berkeley: University of California Press.

Bronfenbrenner, U. (1979a). Contexts of child rearing: Problems and prospects. *American Psychologist, 34,* 844-850.

Bronfenbrenner, U. (1979b). *The ecology of human development.* Cambridge, MA: Harvard University Press.

Bronfenbrenner, U. (1986). Ecology of the family as a context for human development: Research perspectives. *Developmental Psychology, 22,* 723-742.

Bronfenbrenner, U. (1989). Ecological systems theory. In R. Vasta (Ed.), *Annals of child development* (Vol. 6) pp. 187-251. Greenwich, CT: JAI.

Brown, S. (1995). Concepts of childhood and play: An interview with Brian Sutton-Smith. *ReVision, 17,* 35-43.

Bryan, J. (1975). Children's cooperation and helping behaviors. In E. Hetherington (Ed.), *Review of child development research* (Vol. 5, pp. 127-181). Chicago: University of Chicago Press.

Butler, B., & Turner, D. (1987). *Children and anthropological research.* New York: Plenum.

Caldera, Y., Huston, A., & O'Brien, M. (1989). Social interactions and actions and play patterns of parents and toddlers with feminine, masculine and neutral toys. *Child Development, 60,* 70-76.

Cassell, J. (1987). *Children in the field.* Philadelphia: Temple University Press.

Chafe, W. (1992). Women and American society. In L. Luedtke (Ed.), *Making America: The society and culture of the United States* (pp. 327-340). Chapel Hill: University of North Carolina Press.

Chagnon, N. (1977). *Yanomamo: The fierce people.* New York: Holt, Rinehart & Winston.

Chen, S. (1996). Positive childishness: Images of childhood in Japan. In C. Hwang, M. Lamb, & I. Sigel (Eds.), *Images of childhood* (pp. 113-127). Mahwah, NJ: Lawrence Erlbaum.

Chick, G., & Barnett, L. (1995). Children's play and adult leisure. In A. Pellegrini (Ed.), *The future of play theory* (pp. 45-72). Albany: State University of New York Press.

Clark, A., Hocevar, D., & Dembo, M. (1980). The role of cognitive development in children's preferences for skin color. *Developmental Psychology, 16,* 332-339.

Clifford, G. (1989). Man/woman/teacher: Gender, family, and career in American educational history. In D. Warren (Ed.), *American teachers: Histories of a profession at work* (pp. 293-343). New York: Macmillan.

Clifford, J. (1983). On ethnographic authority. *Representations, 1,* 118-146.

Clifford, J. (1988). *The predicament of culture.* Cambridge, MA: Harvard University Press.

Codere, H. (1986). Fieldwork in Rwanda, (1959-1960). In P. Golde (Ed.), *Women in the field: Anthropological experiences* (pp. 143-164). Berkeley: University of California Press.

Cohen, D. (1990, September 19). Early childhood educators bemoan the scarcity of males in teaching. *Education Week,* pp. 12-13.

Coleman, J. (1961). *The adolescent society.* New York: Free Press.

Collins, W. (1984). *Development during middle childhood: The years from six to twelve.* Washington, DC: National Academy Press.

Connor, K. (1989). Aggression: Is it in the eye of the beholder? *Play & Culture, 2,* 213-217.

Corenblum, B., & Wilson, A. (1982). Ethnic preference and identification among Canadian Indian and white children: Replication and extension. *Canadian Journal of Behavioral Science, 14,* 50-59.

Corsaro, W. (1985). *Friendship and peer culture in the early years.* Norwood, NJ: Ablex.

Corsaro, W., & Eder, D. (1990). Children's peer cultures. *Annual Review of Sociology, 16,* 197-220.

Corsino, L. (1987). Fieldworker blues: Emotional stress and research under-involvement in fieldwork settings. *The Social Science Journal, 24,* 275-285.

Cunningham, B. (1992a). "I want to be a teacher, so now what do I do?" In B. Nelson & B. Sheppard (Eds.), *Men in child care and early education: A handbook for administrators and educators.* Stillwater, MN: Nu ink Press.

Cunningham, B. (1992b). Portraying fathers and other men in the curriculum. *Young Children, 49,* 4-13.

Dahawy, B. (1993). *Preschool education in Egypt, Oman, and Japan: A comparative perspective.* (ERIC Document Reproduction Service No. ED 360224)

Daly, A. (1992). The fit between qualitative research and characteristics of families. In J. Gilgun, K. Daly, & G. Handel (Eds.), *Qualitative methods in family research* (pp. 3-11). Newbury Park, CA: Sage.

Davies, L. (1994). *Qualitative approaches in educational research.* Birmingham, AL: University of Birmingham, School of Education.

Davis, D. (1986). Changing self-image: Studying menopausal women in a Newfoundland fishing village. In T. Whitehead & M. Conaway (Eds.), *Self, sex, and gender in cross-cultural fieldwork* (pp. 240-261). Urbana: University of Illinois Press.

Day, B. (1988). What's happening in early childhood programs across the United States? In C. Warger (Ed.), *A resource guide to public school early childhood programs* (pp. 3-31). Alexandria, VA: Association for Supervision and Curriculum Development.

Deal, T., & Peterson, K. (1990). *The principal's role in shaping school culture.* Washington, DC: Department of Education, Office of Educational Research and Improvement.

Delamont, S. (1991). *Fieldwork in educational settings: Methods, pitfalls, and perspectives.* New York: Falmer.

Denby, R. & Alford, K. (1996). Understanding African American discipline styles: Suggestions for effective social work intervention. *Journal of Multicultural Social Work, 4,* 81-98.

Denzin, N. (1996). *Interpretive ethnography.* Thousand Oaks, CA: Sage.

Denzin, N., & Lincoln, Y. (1994). *Handbook of qualitative research.* Thousand Oaks, CA: Sage.

DePietro, J. (1981). Rough-and-tumble play: A function of gender. *Developmental Psychology, 17,* 50-58.

Dion, K., & Dion, K. (1993). Individualistic and collectivist perspectives on gender and the cultural context of love and intimacy. *Journal of Social Issues, 49,* 53-69.

Divale, W. (1976). Female status and cultural evolution: A study in ethnographer bias. *Behavior Science Research, 11,* 169-212.

Dougherty, J. (1985). *Directions in cognitive anthropology.* Chicago: University of Illinois Press.

Draper, H. (1988). *Studying children: Observing and participating.* Mission Hills, CA: Glencoe.

Draper, T., & Gordon, T. (1984). Ichabod Crane in day care: Prospective child care professionals' concerns about male caregivers. *Academic Psychology Bulletin, 6,* 301-308.

Durodoye, B. (1995). Learning styles and the African American student. *Education, 116,* 241-248.

Dwyer, D. (1978). *Images and self images: Male and female in Morocco.* New York: Columbia University Press.

Dwyer, K. (1982). *Moroccan dialogues: Anthropology in question.* Baltimore: Johns Hopkins University Press.

Egertson, H. (1987, May 20). Recapturing kindergarten for 5-year-olds. *Education Week,* pp. 19, 28.

Eisenberg, N. (1983). Sex-typed toys choices: What do they signify? In M. Liss (Ed.), *Social and cognitive skills: Sex roles and children's play* (pp. 45-70). New York: Academic Press.

Eisenberg, N., Murray, E., & Hite, T. (1982). Children's reasoning regarding sex-typed toy choices. *Child Development, 53,* 81-86.

Eisenberg, N., Wolchik, S., Hernandez, R., & Pasternak, J. (1985). Parental socialization of young children's play. *Child Development, 56*, 1506-1513.

Elkind, D. (1981). *The hurried child.* Reading, MA: Addison-Wesley.

Elkind, D. (1987). *Miseducation: Preschoolers at risk.* New York: Knopf.

Elkind, D. (1995). The young child in the postmodern world. *Dimensions of Early Childhood, Spring, 23*(3), 6-9, 39.

Ellis, C. (1995). Emotional and ethical quagmires in returning to the field. *Journal of Contemporary Ethnography, 24*, 68-98.

Ember, C. (1994). Improvements in cross-cultural research methods. *Cross-Cultural Research, 28*, 364-370.

Ember, C. (Ed.) (in press). *Cross-cultural methods for social science.* New Jersey: Prentice Hall.

Ember, C., & Ember, M. (1988). *Anthropology* (5th ed.). Englewood Cliffs, NJ: Prentice Hall.

Engel, J. (1988). Work values of American and Japanese men. *Journal of Social Behavior and Personality, 3*, 191-200.

England, K. (1994). Getting personal: Reflexivity, positionality, and feminist research. *The Professional Geographer, 46*, 80-89.

Erikson, E. (1963). *Childhood and society.* New York: Norton.

Erikson, E. (1968). *Identity: Youth and crisis.* New York: Norton.

Etaugh, C. (1983). Introduction: The influence of environmental factors on sex differences in children's play. In M. Liss (Ed.), *Social and cognitive skills: Sex roles and children's play.* New York: Academic Press.

Fagot, B., Hagan, R., Leinbach, M., & Kronsberg, S. (1985). Differential reactions to assertive and communicative acts of toddler boys and girls. *Child Development, 56*, 1499-1505.

Faller, K., & Everson, M. (1996). Introduction to child interviewing, Part 2. *Child Maltreatment, 1*, 187-189.

Fedigan, L., & Fedigan, L. (1989). Gender and the study of primates. In S. Morgen (Ed.), *Gender and anthropology* (pp. 41-64). Washington, DC: American Anthropological Association.

Fee, E. (1986). Critiques of modern science: The relationship of feminism to other radical epistemologies. In R. Bleier (Ed.), *Feminist approaches to science* (pp. 42-56). New York: Pergamon.

Fetterman, D. (1989). *Ethnography: Step by step.* Newbury Park, CA: Sage.

Finch, J. (1984). It's great to have someone to talk to: The ethics and politics of interviewing women. In C. Bell & H. Roberts (Eds.), *Social researching—Politics, problems, and practice.* London: Routledge & Kegan Paul.

Fine, G. (1987). *With the boys: Little League baseball and preadolescent culture.* Chicago, IL: Chicago University Press.

Fine, G., & Sandstrom, S. (1988). *Knowing children: Participant observation with minors.* Newbury Park, CA: Sage.

Finkelstein, B. (1985). Casting networks of good influence: The reconstruction of childhood in the United States, 1790-1870. In J. Hawes & N. Hiner (Eds.), *American childhood: A research guide and historical handbook* (pp. 111-152). Westport, CT: Greenwood.

Fischer, A. (1986). Field work in five cultures. In P. Golde (Ed.), *Women in the field: Anthropological experiences* (pp. 267-289). Berkeley: University of California Press.

Fiske, S. (1988). *Self, sex, and gender in cross-cultural fieldwork.* Chicago: University of Illinois Press.

Fossey, D. (1983). *Gorillas in the mist.* Boston: Houghton Mifflin.

Franklin, J. (1988). A historical note on black families. In H. McAdoo (Ed.), *Black families* (pp. 23-26). Newbury Park, CA: Sage.

Freud, S. (1900). The interpretation of dreams. *Collected works* (Vol. 4). London: Hogarth.

Freud, S. (1905). Three essays on the theory of sexuality. *Collected works* (Vol. 7). London: Hogarth.

Friedl, E. (1986). Field work in a Greek village. In P. Golde (Ed.), *Women in the field: Anthropological experiences* (pp. 195-236). Berkeley: University of California Press.

Fry, D. (1990). Play aggression among Zapotec children: Implications for the practice hypothesis. *Aggressive Behavior, 16,* 321-340.

Gambell, T. (1995). Ethnography as veneration. *Alberta Journal of Educational Research, 41,* 162-174.

Garbarino, J. (1978, August). The impact of social change on children and youth. *Vital Issues, 27,* 57-74.

Garbarino, J. (1986). Can American families afford the luxury of childhood? *Child Welfare, 65,* 119-128.

Gardner, H. (1987). *The mind's new science: A history of the cognitive revolution.* Cambridge, MA: Harvard University Press.

Gardner, H. (1993). *Frames of mind: A theory of multiple intelligences* (10th ed.). Cambridge, MA: Harvard University Press.

Gee, J. (1989). The narrativization of experience in the oral style. *Journal of Education, 171,* 75-96.

Geiger, S. (1990). What's so feminist about doing women's oral history. *Journal of Women's History, 2,* 169-182.

Gelb, S., & Bishop, K. (1992). Contested terrain: Early childhood education in the United States. In G. Woodill, J. Bernhard, & L. Prochner (Eds.), *International handbook of early childhood education* (pp. 503-528). New York: Garland.

Gesell, A., & Ilg, F. (1946). *The child from five to ten.* New York: Harper & Row

Gilligan, C. (1982). *In a different voice: Psychological theory and women's development.* Cambridge, MA: Harvard University Press.

Gilmore, D. (1991). Subjectivity and subjugation: Fieldwork in the stratified community. *Human Organization, 50,* 215-224.

Goffman, E. (1961). *Asylums: Essays on the social situation of mental patients and other inmates.* Garden City, NY: Anchor.

Golde, P. (1986). *Women in the field: Anthropological experiences* (2nd ed.). Chicago: Aldine.

Goldstein, J. (1996). Aggressive toy play. In A. Pellegrini (Ed.), *The future of play theory: A multidisciplinary inquiry into the contributions of Brian Sutton-Smith* (pp. 127-150). Albany: State University of New York Press.

Gonzalez, N. (1986). The anthropologist as female head of household. In T. Whitehead & M. Conaway (Eds.), *Self, sex, and gender in cross-cultural fieldwork* (pp. 84-100). Urbana: University of Illinois Press.

Goodall, J. (1986). *The chimpanzees of Gombe: Patterns of behavior.* Cambridge, MA: Belknap.

Goodenough, W. (1956). Residence rules. *Southwestern Journal of Anthropology, 12,* 22-37.

Goodenough, W. (1957). Cultural anthropology and linguistics. In P. Garvin (Ed.), *Report of the seventh annual round table meeting on linguistics and language study.* Washington, DC: Georgetown University.

Goodlad, J. (1984). *A place called school: Prospects for the future.* New York: McGraw-Hill.

Goodman, J. (1992). *Elementary schooling for critical democracy.* Albany: State University of New York Press.

Goodwin, M. (1990). *He-said-she-said: Talk as social organization among black children.* Bloomington: Indiana University Press.

Goodwin, M. (1997). Children's linguistic and social worlds. *Anthropology Newsletter, 38,* 1-5.

Granucci, P. (1990). Kindergarten teachers: Working through our identity crisis. *Young Children, 45,* 6-11.

Graue, M., & Walsh, D. (in press). *Children in context: Theories, methods, and ethics of studying children.* Thousand Oaks, CA: Sage.

Greenstock, J., & Pipe, M. (1996). Interviewing children about past events: The influence of peer support and misleading questions. *Child Abuse and Neglect, 20,* 69-80.

Groos, K. (1901). *The play of man.* New York: Appleton.

Guerra, M. (1989). Verbal swaggering: Lunchtime grotesqueries in the child care center. *Play & Culture, 2,* 197-202.

Hale, J. (1986). *Black children: Their roots, culture and learning styles.* Baltimore: Johns Hopkins University Press.

Hale, J. (1991). The transmission of cultural values to young African American children. *Young Children, 46,* 7-15.

Hall, A., & Lin, M. (1995). Theory and practice of children's rights: Implications for mental health counselors. *Journal of Mental Health Counseling, 17,* 63-80.

Hareven, T. (1992). Continuity and change in American family life. In L. Luedtke (Ed.), *Making America: The society and culture of the United States* (pp. 308-327). Chapel Hill: University of North Carolina Press.

Harkness, S. (1996). Anthropological images of childhood. In C. Hwang, M. Lamb, & I. Sigel (Eds.), *Images of childhood* (pp. 36-46). Mahwah, NJ: Lawrence Erlbaum.

Hastrup, K. (1992). Writing ethnography: State of the art. In J. Okely & H. Callaway (Eds.), *Anthropology and autobiography* (pp. 116-133). New York: Routledge.

Hawes, J., & Hiner, N. (Eds.). (1985). *American childhood: A research guide and historical handbook.* Westport, CT: Greenwood.

Heaton, K. (1983). *A study of rough-and-tumble play and serious aggression in preschool children.* Unpublished bachelor's thesis, University of Sheffield, England.

Heider, K. (1988). The Roshomon effect: When ethnographers disagree. *American Anthropologist, 90,* 73-81.

Helms, J. (1993). I also said, "White racial identity influences white researchers." *The Counseling Psychologist, 21,* 240-243.

Herod, A. (1993). Gender issues in the use of interviewing as a research method. *The Professional Geographer, 45,* 305-317.

Holmes, R. (1991). Categories of play: A kindergartner's view. *Play & Culture, 4,* 43-50.

Holmes, R. (1992). Play during snacktime. *Play & Culture, 5,* 295-304.

Holmes, R. (1995). *How young children perceive race.* Thousand Oaks, CA: Sage.

Hsue, Y. (1995). Developmentally appropriate practice and traditional Taiwanese culture. *Journal of Instructional Psychology, 22,* 320-324.

Hughes, F. (1995). *Children, play and development.* Boston: Allyn & Bacon.

Hunt, A., & Prout, J. (Eds.). (1990a). *Constructing and reconstructing childhood.* Bristol, PA: Falmer.

Hunt, A., & Prout, J. (1990b). Re-presenting childhood: Time and transition in the study of childhood. In A. Hunt & J. Prout (Eds.), *Constructing and reconstructing childhood* (pp. 216-237). Bristol, PA: Falmer.

Hunt, J. (1984). The development of rapport through the negotiation of gender in field work among police. *Human Organization, 43,* 283-296.

Hunt, P., & Frankenberg, R. (1990). It's a small world: Disneyland, the family and the multiple re-representations of American childhood. In A. Hunt & J. Prout (Eds.), *Constructing and reconstructing childhood* (pp. 99-117). Bristol, PA: Falmer.

Huntington, G. (1987). Different apron strings: Children as field assistants. *Human Organization, 46,* 83-85.

Hurtado, H. (1992). Preschool education in Argentina. In G. Woodill, J. Bernhard, & L. Prochner (Eds.), *International handbook of early childhood education* (pp. 39-47). New York: Garland.

Huston, A. (1983). Sex typing. In P. Mussen (Ed.), *Handbook of child psychology* (4th ed., Vol. 4, pp. 387-467). New York: John Wiley.

Hwang, C., Lamb, M., & Sigel, I. (1996). *Images of childhood.* Mahwah, NJ: Lawrence Erlbaum.

Jacklin, C. (1992). *The psychology of gender* (Vols. 1-4). New York: New York University Press.

Johnson, J. (1975). *Doing field research.* London: Free Press.

Johnson, N. (1985). *West Haven.* Chapel Hill: University of North Carolina Press.

Johnson, N. (1986). Ethnographic research and rites of incorporation: A sex- and gender-based comparison. In T. Whitehead & M. Conaway (Eds.), *Self, sex, and gender in cross-cultural fieldwork* (pp. 164-181). Urbana: University of Illinois Press.

Julian, T., & McKenry, P. (1994). Cultural variations in parenting. *Family Relations, 43,* 30-38.

Kagan, J. (1971). *Personality development.* New York: Harcourt Brace.

Kagan, J. (1984). *The nature of the child.* New York: Basic Books.

Kakar, S. (1978). *The inner world: A psycho-analytic study of childhood and society in India.* New Delhi: Oxford University Press.

Kashima, Y., Yamaguchi, S., & Kim, U. (1995). Culture, gender, and self: A perspective from individualism-collectivism research. *Journal of Personality and Social Psychology, 69,* 925-937.

Kauppinen-Toropainen, K., & Lammi, J. (1993). Men in female-dominated occupations: A cross-cultural comparison. In C. Williams (Ed.), *Doing "women's work": Men in nontraditional occupations* (pp. 91-112). Newbury Park, CA: Sage.

Keller, E. (1985). *Reflections on gender and science.* New Haven, CT: Yale University Press.

Keller, E. (1987). The gender/science system: Or, is sex to gender as nature is to science? *Hypatia, 2,* 37-59.

Kelly-Byrne, D. (1989). *A child's play life: An ethnographic study.* New York: Teachers College Press.

Kempton, W. (1981). Category grading and taxonomic relations: A mug is a sort of cup. In R. Casson (Ed.), *Language, culture and cognition: Anthropological perspectives* (pp. 203-229). New York: Macmillan.

Kleinman, S., & Copp, M. (1993). *Emotions and fieldwork* (Qualitative Research Methods Series, Vol. 28). Newbury Park, CA: Sage.

Kohlberg, L. (1966). A cognitive-developmental analysis of children's sex-role concepts and attitudes. In E. Maccoby (Ed.), *The development of sex differences.* Stanford, CA: Stanford University Press.

Kohlberg, L. (1968, April). The child as moral philosopher. *Psychology Today,* 25-30.

Kohlberg, L. (1981). *Essays on moral development.* San Francisco: Harper & Row.

Konner, M. (1991). *Childhood.* Boston: Little, Brown.

Kulick, D. (1995). The sexual life of anthropologists: Erotic subjectivity and ethnographic work. In D. Kulick & M. Wilson (Eds.), *Taboo: Sex, identity and erotic subjectivity in anthropological fieldwork* (pp. 1-28). London: Routledge.

Kulick, D., & Wilson, M. (Eds.). (1995). *Taboo: Sex, identity and erotic subjectivity in anthropological fieldwork.* London: Routledge.

Laing, Z., & Pang, L. (1992). Early childhood education in the Peoples' Republic of China. In G. Woodill, J. Bernhard, & L. Prochner (Eds.), *International handbook of early childhood education* (pp. 169-174). New York: Garland.

Lamb, M. (1981). The development of father-infant relationships. In M. Lamb (Ed.), *The role of the father in child development* (pp. 1-70). New York: John Wiley.

Lamb, M. (1987). Introduction: The emergent father. In M. Lamb (Ed.), *The father's role: Cross-cultural perspectives* (pp. 3-25). Hillsdale, NJ: Lawrence Erlbaum.

Langlois, J., & Downs, A. (1980). Mothers, fathers, and peers as socialization agents of sex-typed play behaviors in young children. *Child Development, 51*, 1217-1247.

Lasater, C., & Johnson, J. (1994). Culture, play, and early childhood education. In J. Roopnarine, J. Johnson, & F. Hooper (Eds.), *Children's play in diverse cultures* (pp. 210-228). Albany: State University of New York Press.

Leavitt, R. (1994). *Power and emotion in infant-toddler day care.* Albany: State University of New York Press.

Lesko, N. (1988). *Symbolizing society: Stories, rites and structure in a Catholic high school.* New York: Falmer.

Lewis, C. (1986). Children's social development in Japan: Research directions. In H. Stevenson, H. Azuma, & K. Hakuta (Eds.), *Child development and education in Japan* (pp. 186-200). New York: Freeman.

Liebow, E. (1967). *Tally's corner: A study of Negro street-corner men.* Boston: Little, Brown.

Loftus, E. (1975). Leading questions and the eyewitness report. *Cognitive Psychology, 7*, 560-572.

Loftus, E. (1991). *Witness for the defense: The accused, the eyewitness, and the expert who puts memory on trial.* New York: St. Martin's.

Loftus, E., & Zanni, G. (1975). Eyewitness testimony: The influence of the wording of a question. *Bulletin of the Psychonomic Society, 5*, 86-88.

Logan, S. (1996). A strength's perspective on black families: Then and now. In S. Logan (Ed.), *The black family* (pp. 8-20). Boulder, CO: Westview .

Lynott, P., & Logue, B. (1993). The "hurried child": The myth of lost childhood in contemporary American society. *Sociological Forum, 8*, 471-491.

Maccoby, E. (1986). Social groupings in childhood: Their relationship to prosocial and antisocial behavior in boys and girls. In D. Olweus, J. Block, & M. Radye-Yarrow (Eds.), *Development of antisocial and prosocial behavior: Research, theory, and issues* (pp. 263-280). New York: Academic Press.

Maccoby, E. (1990). Gender and relationships: A developmental account. *American Psychologist, 45,* 513-520.

Maccoby, E. (1992). The role of parents in the socialization of children: An historical overview. *Developmental Psychology, 28,* 1006-1017.

Maccoby, E., & Jacklin, C. (1974). *The psychology of sex differences.* Palo Alto, CA: Stanford University Press.

Maccoby, E., & Jacklin, C. (1987). Gender segregation in childhood. In H. Reese (Ed.), *Advances in child development and behavior* (Vol. 20, pp. 239-287). Boston: Academic Press.

MacDonald, K. (1993). *Parent-child play: Descriptions and implications.* Albany: State University of New York Press.

Mandell, S. (1988). The least adult role in studying children. *Journal of Contemporary Ethnography, 16,* 433-467.

Mason, J. (1996). *Qualitative researching.* Thousand Oaks, CA: Sage.

McGrew, W. (1972). *An ethological study of children's behavior.* New York: Academic Press.

McKeganey, N., & Bloor, M. (1991). Spotting the invisible man: the influence of male gender on fieldwork relations. *British Journal of Sociology, 42,* 195-210.

McLean, S., Piscitelli, B., Halliwell, G., & Ashby, F. (1992). Australian early childhood education. In G. Woodill, J. Bernhard, & L. Prochner (Eds.), *International handbook of early childhood education* (pp. 49-73). New York: Garland.

Mead, M. (1961). *Coming of age in Samoa* (3rd ed.). New York: Morrow Quill.

Mead, M. (1962). *The school in American culture: The Inglis lecture 1950.* Cambridge, MA: Harvard University Press.

Mead, M. (1986). Field work in Pacific Islands, 1925-1967. In P. Golde (Ed.), *Women in the field: Anthropological experiences* (pp. 293-331). Berkeley: University of California Press.

Mervis, C. (1987). Child basic object categories and early lexical development. In U. Neisser (Ed.), *Concepts and conceptual development: Ecological and intellectual factors in categorization* (pp. 201-233). Cambridge, UK: Cambridge University Press.

Middleton, J. (1970). *From child to adult: Studies in the anthropology of education.* Garden City, NY: Natural History Press.

Morgen, S. (Ed). (1989). *Gender and anthropology: Critical reviews for research and teaching.* Washington, DC: American Anthropological Association.

Murphy, Y., & Murphy, R. (1974). *Women of the forest.* New York: Columbia University Press.

Murphy, Y., & Murphy, R. (1985). *Women of the forest.* New York: Columbia University Press.

Nast, H. (1994). Women in the field: Critical feminist methodologies and theoretical perspectives. *The Professional Geographer, 46,* 54-66.

Nobles, W. (1988). African-American family life: An instrument of culture. In H. McAdoo (Ed.), *Black families* (pp. 44-53). Newbury Park, CA: Sage.

Oakley, A. (1981). Interviewing women: A contradiction in terms. In H. Roberts (Ed.), *Doing feminist research.* London: Routledge Kegan Paul.

Oakley, A. (1994). Women and children first and last: Parallels and differences between children's and women's studies. In B. Mayall (Ed.), *Children's childhoods: Observed and experienced* (pp. 13-32). London: Falmer.

Opie, I., & Opie, P. (1984). *Children's games in street and playground.* Oxford: Oxford University Press.

Orbe, M. (1995). African American communication research: Toward a deeper understanding of interethnic communication. *Western Journal of Communication, 59,* 61-79.

Packard, V. (1983). *Our endangered children: Growing up in a changing world.* Boston: Little, Brown.

Parke, R., & Tinsley, B. (1987). Family interaction in infancy. In J. Osofsky (Ed.), *Handbook of infant development* (2nd ed.). New York: John Wiley.

Pass, C. (1987). Qualitative research will enhance the care of children. *Children's Health Care, 15,* 214-215.

Patton, M. (1990). *Qualitative evaluation and research methods.* Newbury Park, CA: Sage.

Pedersen, P. (1993). The multicultural dilemma of white cross-cultural researchers. *The Counseling Psychologist, 21,* 229-232.

Pellegrini, A. (1985). Social-cognitive aspects of children's play: The effects of age, gender, and activity centers. *Journal of Applied Developmental Psychology, 6,* 129-140.

Pellegrini, A. (1988). Elementary-school children's rough and tumble play and social competence. *Developmental Psychology, 24,* 802-806.

Pellegrini, A. (1989). So, what about recess? *Play & Culture, 2,* 354-356.

Pellegrini, A. (1996). *Observing children in their natural worlds: A methodological primer.* Mahwah, NJ: Lawrence Erlbaum.

Pelto, P., & Pelto, G. (1978). *Anthropological research: The structure of inquiry* (2nd ed.). New York: Cambridge University Press.

Peshkin, A. (1982). The researcher and subjectivity: Reflections on an ethnography of school and community. In G. Spindler (Ed.), *Doing the ethnography of schooling: Educational anthropology in action* (pp. 48-67). New York: Holt, Rinehart & Winston.

Peshkin, A. (1988). In search of subjectivity: One's own. *Educational Researcher, 17,* 17-22.

Peters, M. (1988). Parenting in black families with young children: A historical perspective. In H. McAdoo (Ed.)., *Black families* (pp. 228-241). Newbury Park, CA: Sage.

Piaget, J. (1929). *The child's conception of the world.* New York: Harcourt Brace.

Piaget, J. (1959). *The language and thought of the Child* (M. Gabain, trans.). London: Routledge & Kegan Paul.

Piaget, J. (1963). *The origins of intelligence in children.* New York: Nonon.

Plumbo, M. (1995). Living in two different worlds or living in the world differently. *Journal of Holistic Nursing, 13,* 155-174.

Postman, N. (1982). *The disappearance of childhood.* New York: Delacorte.

Rane, T., & Draper, T. (1995). Negative evaluations of mens' nurturant touching of young children. *Psychological Reports, 7,* 811-818.

Reifel, S. (1986). Play in the elementary school cafeteria. In B. Mergen (Ed.), *Cultural dimensions of play, games, and sport* (pp. 29-36). Champaign, IL: Human Kinetics.

Reinharz, S. (1992). *Feminist methods in social research.* New York: Oxford University Press.

Renshaw, P. (1981). The roots of current peer interaction research: A historical analysis of the 1930s. In S. Asher & J. Gottman (Eds.), *The development of children's friendships* (pp. 1-28). Cambridge, UK: Cambridge University Press.

Rivkin, M. (1995). *The great outdoors: Restoring children's right to play outside.* Washington, DC: National Association for the Education of Young Children.

Rizzo, T. (1989). *Friendship development among children in school.* Norwood, NJ: Ablex.

Robinson, B. (1988). Vanishing breed: Men in child care programs. *Young Children, 43,* 54-58.

Robinson, C., & Morris, J. (1986). The gender stereotyped nature of Christmas toys by 36-, 48-, and 60-month-old children: A comparison between non-requested vs. requested toys. *Sex Roles, 15,* 21-32.

Roopnarine, J., & Hossain, Z. (1992). Parent-child interactions in urban Indian families in New Delhi: Are they changing? In J. Roopnarine & D. Carter (Eds.), *Parent-child socialization in diverse cultures* (pp. 1-16). Norwood, NJ: Ablex.

Roopnarine, J., Hossain, Z., Gill, P., & Brophy, H. (1994). Play in the East Indian context. In J. Roopnarine, J. Johnson, & F. Hooper (Eds.), *Children's play in diverse cultures* (pp. 9-30). Albany: State University of New York Press.

Roopnarine, J., Johnson, J., & Hooper, F. (Eds.). (1994). *Children's play in diverse cultures.* Albany, NY: State University of New York Press.

Roopnarine, J., Talukder, E., Jain, D., Joshi, P., & Srivastav, P. (1990). Characteristics of holding, patterns of play and social behaviors between parents and infants in New Delhi, India. *Developmental Psychology, 26,* 867-873.

Rosaldo, R. (1989). *Culture and truth: The remaking of social analysis.* Boston: Beacon.

Rosch, E. (1973). On the internal structure of perceptual and semantic categories. In T. Moore (Ed.), *Cognitive development and the acquisition of language* (pp. 111-144). New York: Academic Press.

Rowell, T. (1984). Introduction to section 1: Mothers, infants, and adolescents. In M. Small (Ed.), *Female primates: Studies by women primatologists* (pp. 13-16). New York: Alan R. Liss.

Rubin, K., Fein, G., & Vandenberg, B. (1983). Play. In P. Mussen (Ed.), *Handbook of child psychology* (4th ed., pp. 693-774). New York: John Wiley.

Ruiz, N. (1995). The social construction of ability and disability: Optimal and at-risk lessons in a bilingual classroom. *Journal of Learning Disabilities, 28,* 491-503.

Rury, J. (1989). Who became teachers? The social characteristics of teachers in American history. In D. Warren (Ed.), *American teachers: Histories of a profession at work* (pp. 9-48). New York: Macmillan.

Rutter, M., Maugham, B., Mortimore, P., & Ouston, J. (1979). *Fifteen thousand hours: Secondary school and their effect on children.* London: Open Books.

Sabbaghian, Z. (1992). Kindergarten and primary school education in Iran. In G. Woodill, J. Bernhard, & L. Prochner (Eds.), *International handbook of early childhood education* (pp. 299-305). New York: Garland.

Sanjek, R. (Ed.). (1990). *Fieldnotes: The making of anthropology.* Ithaca, NY: Cornell University Press.

Schickedanz, J. (1994). Early childhood education and school reform: Consideration of some philosophic barriers. *Journal of Education, 176,* 29-48.

Schneider, D. (1995). *American childhood: Risks and realities.* New Brunswick, NJ: Rutgers University Press.

Schofield, J. (1981). Complimentary and conflicting identities: Images and interaction in an interracial school. In S. Asher & J. Gottman (Eds.), *The development of children's friendships* (pp. 53-92). Cambridge, UK: Cambridge University Press.

Schofield, J. (1989). *Black and white in school: Trust, tension, or tolerance?* New York: Teachers College Press.

Schwartz, L., & Markham, W. (1985). Sex stereotyping in children's toy advertisements. *Sex Roles, 12,* 157-170.

Schwartz, T. (Ed.). (1976). *Socialization as cultural communication: Development of theme in the work of Margaret Mead.* Berkeley: University of California Press.

Schwartzman, H. (1978). *Transformations.* New York: Plenum.

Schwartzman, H. (1995). Representing children's play: Anthropologists at work. In A. Pellegrini (Ed.), *The future of play theory* (pp. 243-256). Albany: State University of New York Press.

Scott-Jones, D. (1994). Ethical issues in reporting and referring in research with low-income minority children [Special issue: Reporting and referring child and adolescent research participants]. *Ethics and Behavior, 4,* 97-108.

Segall, M., Dasen, P., Berry, J., & Poortinga, Y. (1990). *Human behavior in global perspective.* Boston: Allyn & Bacon.

Serpell, R. (1996). Cultural models of childhood in indigenous socialization and formal schooling in Zambia. In C. Hwang, M. Lamb, & I. Sigel (Eds.), *Images of childhood* (pp. 129-142). Mahwah, NJ: Lawrence Erlbaum.

Sexton, P. (1982). *The new nightingales: Hospital workers, unions, new women's issues.* New York: Enquiry.

Shaffir, W., & Stebbins, R. (Eds.). (1991). *Experiencing fieldwork.* Newbury Park, CA: Sage.

Shaffir, W., Stebbins, R., & Turowetz, A. (1980). *Fieldwork experience.* New York: St. Martin's.

Shu-Min, Huang. (1996). Nutritional well-being of preschool children in a North China village. *Modern China, 22,* 355-371.

Sieber, B., & Sieber, J. (1992). *Social research on children and adolescents: Ethical issues.* Newbury Park, CA: Sage.

Siegal, M. (1987). Are sons and daughters treated more differently by fathers than by mothers. *Developmental Review, 7,* 183-209.

Skeen, P., Robinson, B., & Coleman, M. (1986). Gender-role attitudes of professional female educators toward men in early childhood education. *Psychological Reports, 59,* 723-730.

Skelton, C. (1996). Learning to be "tough": The fostering of maleness in the primary school. *Gender and Education, 8,* 185-199.

Sluckin, A. (1981). *Growing up in the playground: The social development of children.* London: Routledge & Kegan Paul.

Smith, H. (1996). Building on the strengths of black families: Self-help and empowerment. In S. Logan (Ed.), *The black family* (pp. 21-38). Boulder, CO: Westview.

Spence, J. (1985). Achievement American style: The rewards and costs of individualism. *American Psychologist, 40,* 1285-1295.

Spindler, G. (1970). *Being an anthropologist: Fieldwork in eleven cultures.* New York: Holt, Rinehart & Winston.

Spindler, G., & Spindler, L. (1983). Anthropologists view American culture. *Annual Review of Anthropology, 12,* 49-78.

Spindler, G., & Spindler, L. (1990). *The American cultural dialogue and its transmission.* London: Falmer.

Spradley, J. (1980). *Participant observation.* New York: Holt, Rinehart & Winston.

Stack, C. (1974). *All our kin.* New York: Harper & Row.

Stack, C. (1996). Writing ethnography: Feminist critical practice. In D. Wolf (Ed.), *Feminist dilemmas in fieldwork* (pp. 96-106). Boulder, CO: Westview.

Stevenson, H., Azuma, H., & Hakuta, K. (1986). *Child development and education in Japan.* New York: Freeman.

Steward, M., Bussey, K., Goodman, G., & Saywitz, K. (1993). Implications of developmental research for interviewing children [Special issue: Clinical recognition of sexually abused children]. *Child Abuse and Neglect, 17,* 25-37.

Sudarkasa, N. (1986). In a world of women: Field work in a Yoruba community. In P. Golde (Ed.), *Women in the field: Anthropological experiences* (pp. 167-191). Berkeley: University of California Press.

Sudarkasa, N. (1988). Interpreting African heritage in Afro-American family organization. In H. McAdoo (Ed.), *Black families* (pp. 27-43). Newbury Park, CA: Sage.

Sue, D. (1993). Confronting ourselves: The white and racial/ethnic minority researcher. *The Counseling Psychologist, 21,* 244-249.

Super, C., & Harkness, S. (1986). The developmental niche: A conceptualization at the interface of society and the individual. *International Journal of Behavioral Development, 9,* 545-570.

Suppal, P., Roopnarine, J., Buesig, T., & Bennet, A. (1996). Ideological beliefs about family practices: Contemporary perspectives among North Indian families. *International Journal of Psychology, 31,* 29-37.

Sutton-Smith, B. (1979). The play of girls. In C. Koop (Ed.), *Becoming female: Perspectives on development* (pp. 229-257). New York: Plenum.

Sutton-Smith, B. (1981). *The folkstories of children.* Philadelphia: University of Pennsylvania Press.

Sutton-Smith. B. (1988). War toys and childhood aggression. *Play & Culture, 1,* 57-69.

Sutton-Smith, B. (1990). School playground as festival. *Children's Environments Quarterly, 7,* 3-7.

Sutton-Smith, B. (1994). A memory of games and some games of memory. In J. Lee (Ed.), *Life before story: The autobiographies of psychologists from a narrative perspective* (pp. 125-142). New York: Praeger.

Sutton-Smith, B. (Ed.). (1995). *Children's folklore: A source book.* New York: Garland.

Tabu, M., & Aoki, H. (1990). *Early childhood education in Japan* (NIER Occasional Paper). Tokyo: National Institute for Educational Research. (ERIC Document Reproduction Service No. ED 329332)

Tajfel, H. (1982). Social psychology of intergroup relations. *Annual Review of Psychology, 33,* 1-39.

Takeuchi, M. (1994). Children's play in Japan. In J. Roopnarine, J. Johnson, & F. Hooper (Eds.), *Children's play in diverse cultures* (pp. 51-72). Albany: State University of New York Press.

Taylor, I., et al. (1994). *The internalization of values: Adopting cooperation (Sunao) in Japanese preschools.* (ERIC Document Reproduction Service No. ED 374032)

Thorne, B. (1993). *Gender play: Boys and girls at school.* New Brunswick, NJ: Rutgers University Press.

Tobin, D., Wu, D., & Davidson, D. (1989). *Preschool in three cultures.* Cambridge, MA: Harvard University Press.

Top 10 signs of a good kindergarten classroom. (1996). *Brown University Child & Adolescent Behavior Letter, 12,* 4.

Tracy, D. (1987). Toys, spatial ability, and science and mathematics achievement: Are they related? *Sex Roles, 17,* 115-138.

Triandis, H. (1989). The self and social behavior in differing cultural contexts. *Psychological Review, 96,* 506-520.

Triandis, H., & Berry, J. (Eds.). (1981). *Handbook of cross-cultural psychology* (Vol. 1). Boston: Allyn & Bacon.

Triandis, H., Brislin, R., & Hui, R. (1988). Cross-cultural training across the individualism-collectivism divide. *International Journal of Intercultural Relations, 12,* 269-289.

Turnbull, C. (1968). *The forest people.* New York: Simon & Schuster.

Turner, V., & Bruner, E. (1986). *The anthropology of experience.* Urbana: University of Illinois Press.

Tyler, S. (1969). *Cognitive anthropology.* New York: Holt, Rinehart & Winston.

Tylor, E. (1958). *Primitive culture.* New York: Harper Torchbooks. (Original work published in 1871)

Van Maanen, J. (1988). *Tales of the field: On writing ethnography.* Chicago: University of Chicago Press.

Van Maanen, J. (Ed.). (1995). *Representational challenges in ethnography.* Thousand Oaks, CA: Sage.

Wade, P. (1993). Sexuality and masculinity in fieldwork among Colombian blacks. In D. Bell, P. Caplan, & W. Karim (Eds.), *Gendered fields: Women, men and ethnography* (pp. 199-214). London: Routledge.

Wagner, J. (1995). Studies of individualism-collectivism: Effects on cooperation in groups. *Academy of Management Journal, 38,* 152-172.

Warren, C. (1988). *Gender issues in field research* (Qualitative Research Methods, Vol. 9). Newbury Park, CA: Sage.

Wegener-Spohring, G. (1989). War toys and aggressive games. *Play & Culture, 2,* 35-47.

Werner O., & Schoepfle, G. (1987). *Systematic fieldwork: Foundations of ethnography and interviewing.* Newbury Park, CA: Sage.

Wescott, H. (1994). On sensitivity and ethical issues in child witness research. *Child Abuse and Neglect, 18,* 287-290.

Wheeler, L., Reis, H., & Bond, M. (1989). Collectivism-individualism in everyday social life: The middle kingdom and the melting pot. *Journal of Personality and Social Psychology, 57,* 79-86.

White, M., & LeVine, R. (1986). What is an Ii ko (Good child)? In H. Stevenson, H. Azuma, & K. Hakuta (Eds.), *Child development and education in Japan* (pp. 55-62). New York: Freeman.

Whitehead, T., & Conaway, M. (1986). *Self, sex and gender in cross-cultural fieldwork*. Urbana: University of Illinois Press.

Whiting, B., & Child, I. (1963). *Six cultures: Studies of childrearing*. New York: John Wiley.

Whiting, B., & Edwards, C. (1973). A cross-cultural analysis of sex differences in the behavior of children aged three through eleven. *Journal of Social Psychology, 91*, 171-188.

Whiting, B., & Whiting, J. (1975). *Children of six cultures: A psycho-cultural analysis*. Cambridge, MA: Harvard University Press.

Williams, B. (1996). Skinfolk, not kinfolk: Comparative reflections on the identity of participant-observation in two field situations. In D. Wolf (Ed.), *Feminist dilemmas in fieldwork* (pp. 72-95). Boulder, CO: Westview.

Williams, C. (1993). *Doing women's work: Men in nontraditional occupations*. Newbury Park, CA: Sage.

Williams, C. (1995). *Still a man's world: Men who do women's work*. Berkeley: University of California Press.

Williams, C., & Heikes, E. (1993). The importance of researcher's gender in the in-depth interview: Evidence from two case studies of male nurses. *Gender and Society, 7*, 280-291.

Williams, J., & Best, D. (1990). *Sex and psyche: Gender and self viewed cross-culturally* (Cross-Cultural Research and Methodology Series, Vol. 13). Newbury Park, CA: Sage.

Winn, M. (1983). *Children without childhood*. New York: Pantheon.

Wolcott, H. (1990). *Writing up qualitative research*. (Qualitative Methods Series, Vol. 20). Newbury Park, CA: Sage.

Wolf, D. (1992). *Factory daughters*. Berkeley: University of California Press.

Wolf, D. (Ed.). (1996a). *Feminist dilemmas in fieldwork*. Boulder, CO: Westview.

Wolf, D. (1996b). Situating feminist dilemmas in fieldwork. In D. Wolf (Ed.), *Feminist dilemmas in fieldwork* (pp. 1-55). Boulder, CO: Westview.

Wolf, J. (1995). *If you haven't been there, you don't know what it's like: Life at Enchanted Gate from the inside*. Unpublished doctoral dissertation, University of Illinois, Urbana-Champaign.

Wolf, M. (1996). Afterword: Musings from an old gray wolf. In D. Wolf (Ed.), *Feminist dilemmas in fieldwork* (pp. 215-222). Boulder, CO: Westview.

Wood, G. (1988). Democracy and the curriculum. In L. Beyer & M. Apple (Eds.), *The curriculum: Problems, politics, and possibilities* (pp. 166-187). Albany: State University of New York Press.

Woodgate, R. (1996). My hurts: Hospitalized young children's perceptions of acute pain. *Qualitative Health Research, 6,* 184-196.

Woodill, G. (1992). International early childhood care and education: Historical perspectives. In G. Woodill, J. Bernhard, & L. Prochner (Eds.), *International handbook of early childhood education* (pp. 3-10). New York: Garland.

Woodill, G., Bernhard, J., & Prochner, L. (1992). *International handbook of early childhood education.* New York: Garland.

Yamamura, Y. (1986). The child in Japanese society. In H. Stevenson, H. Azuma, & K. Hakuta (Eds.), *Child development and education in Japan* (pp. 28-38). New York: Freeman.

Zigler, E. (1987). Formal schooling for four-year-olds? *North American Psychologist, 42,* 254-260.

Index

151

About the Author

Robyn M. Holmes received a PhD in anthropology from Rutgers University. She is Assistant Professor of Psychology at Monmouth University, and approaches children's behavior and cognition from an interdisciplinary perspective. She is the author of *How Young Children Perceive Race,* and she has published numerous articles on children's play, educational practices, and children's social cognition in journals such as *Play & Culture, Education & Treatment of Children,* and *Child Study Journal.* She is a fellow of the American Anthropological Association, and a member of the American Psychological Association, the Association for the Study of Play, and the National Association for the Education of Young Children.